The Loyal Opposition

The Loyal Opposition

Struggling with the Church on Homosexuality

Edited by

TEX SAMPLE & AMY E. DeLONG

ABINGDON PRESS/Nashville

THE LOYAL OPPOSITION:
STRUGGLING WITH THE CHURCH ON HOMOSEXUALITY

Copyright © 2000 by Abingdon Press

This book is printed on recycled, acid-free paper.

Library of Congress Cataloging-in-Publication Data

The loyal opposition : struggling with the church on homosexuality / edited by Tex Sample & Amy E. DeLong.
     p. cm.
     Includes bibliographical references.
     ISBN 0-687-08425-3 (alk. paper)
     1. Homosexuality—Religious aspects—United Methodist Church (U.S.) 2. United Methodist Church (U.S.)—Doctrines. I. Sample, Tex. II. DeLong, Amy E., 1967–

BX8385.H6 L68 2000
261.8'35766—dc21   99-050271

Quotations from the *Discipline* are from *The Book of Discipline of The United Methodist Church—1996*. Copyright © 1996 by The United Methodist Publishing House. Used by permission.

Passages in chapter 4 from "Homosexuality, Marriage and the Church" are copyright © 1998 Christian Century Foundation. Reprinted by permission from the July 1-8, 1998, issue of the *Christian Century*.

Scripture quotations, unless otherwise noted, are from the New Revised Standard Version Bible. Copyright © 1989 by the Division of Christian Education of the National Council of the Churches of Christ in the USA. Used by permission.

Scripture quotations noted RSV are from the Revised Standard Version of the Bible, copyright 1946, 1952, 1971 by the Division of Christian Education of the National Council of the Churches of Christ in the USA. Used by permission.

00 01 02 03 04 05 06 07 08 09 —10 9 8 7 6 5 4 3 2

MANUFACTURED IN THE UNITED STATES OF AMERICA

Contents

HOMOSEXUALITY, RESISTANCE, AND THE SOCIAL PRINCIPLES

RESISTANCE AND HUMAN RIGHTS

LIFE IN THE CHURCH AS RESISTANCE

RESISTANCE AND ECCLESIAL DISOBEDIENCE

Acknowledgments

The writing of books requires relationships, friends, and colleagues. Such is certainly the case in this edited collection of articles. We, the editors, are deeply indebted.

The idea for this book grew out of Amy DeLong's seminary class work with Dr. Toinette Eugene in the winter of 1997. Without Dr. Eugene's guidance the idea for this book would never have been born. In the spring of the same year, Amy had a conversation with the Reverend Greg Dell, in which the question was raised about how one remains faithful to the church while still opposing its position on homosexuality. From that discussion it became clear that loyalty and resistance would be the focus. Amy then contacted Tex Sample to ask him to assist as an editor.

From there we began to ask people to write articles. No one who wrote for us had time to do so, but they did it anyway. They are busy people, but they know how important the inclusiveness of gay and lesbian people is for the church. We, of course, owe the authors a substantial debt of gratitude.

We are further indebted to Margaret Kohl who worked diligently on the manuscript as the typist and who coordinated different computer programs and other arcane technological mysteries. Mary Jane Shewmake provided proofreading services. We are indebted to both for much needed help.

Moreover, each of us is sustained by personal relationships which provide the support and friendship utterly necessary to life and work. Amy is forever grateful to Val Zellmer, Nancy Moffatt, Sue Laurie, Elizabeth Nagel, Steve Briggs, and to Tex (for listening to me in the first place). Tex expresses deep appreciation to Peggy Sample.

We would also be remiss if we did not say a word about our

love and unyielding appreciation for The United Methodist Church, which has nurtured us and taught us about a gracious God. We cannot understand our very lives apart from the people called Methodist. Our love for the Church is deeper than our resistance to it. In fact, our resistance is intrinsic to this love. Our deepest desire certainly is not to injure the Church, but to participate in a deepening of its faithfulness to God, and, indeed, to be more faithful ourselves.

Foreword

Leontine T. C. Kelly

The United Methodist Church is indebted to Amy DeLong and Tex Sample for the book, *The Loyal Opposition: Struggling with the Church on Homosexuality.* They have brought together the clear thinking, historical perspective, scriptural interpretation, doctrinal position, disciplinary process, and the witness of faith of some of United Methodists' most outstanding leaders and scholars.

The loyal oppositionist is the proper name for these distinguished persons who will not accept the status quo as norm for the Church when members are suffering and denied the rights of all. Their loyalty to God supersedes their love for the law of the denomination they have so sacrificially served. I am honored to be asked to write this foreword, and I commend the book to you in its entirety.

As I excitedly read the pages of this important document, I thought of two African American songs: "There's No Hiding Place Down Here," and "I Just Couldn't Keep It to Myself." Love for this Church of ours frees, or should free, persons to share their experiences and understandings, especially since homosexuality is deemed the most controversial issue facing Methodism since slavery split the Church.

One busy morning during my active episcopacy as bishop of The Northern California-Nevada Annual Conference (San Francisco Area), Margaret Wingerd, my secretary, placed a huge stack of letters before me. As usual, she put the "best" letter on top. I can never forget the words I read:

11

Dear Bishop Kelly:

The United Methodist Church cannot "bestow" Sacred
Worth on my daughter, she was born with it! God gave it
to her! While I do not understand her sexual orientation, I
know that I love her and that God loves her.

I deeply regret that the Church that taught her of God's
love for all people should refuse to show her that love and
accept her as a Child of God.

Sincerely yours,
A United Methodist Mother

Most of the letters on the subject of homosexuality stacked
beneath her anguished outcry were filled with hate. They
reflected an understanding of God that was completely foreign
to my Methodist/Christian upbringing. As an African American
woman my faith never blinded me to the fact that the Church I
love makes great social pronouncements which do not, necessarily, lead to practice either in the life of the church or its individual members. Yet the decision-making process of General
Conference has had some integrity for me. Our growth on
issues of social justice moved us along, sometimes by inches,
quadrennium after quadrennium. There is no doubt that our
Social Principles reflect a denomination struggling to interpret
what it means to accept and minister to all humanity—an
acceptance and a ministry that are clearly requirements for disciples of Jesus Christ.

I have told the story so often of being in a Methodist
Episcopal parsonage in Cincinnati, Ohio. There, as children, we
located a tunnel which proved to be a station of the
Underground Railroad. This incident, and my father's interpretation of it, became the theological grounding for my whole life.
I came to understand that who we were in the sight of God was
far different from the racism, segregation, and discrimination
which we experienced. We were children of God! Only a caring
God could weave together a whole system of unrelated persons
in opposition to the powerful institution of slavery. Somebody
preached a clear gospel, which somebody heard and risked act-

ing on. As Dietrich Bonhoeffer reminded us, discipleship is cost-
ly. We were never taught to hate, no matter what. We learned
early on to "reach and teach." Younger generations are still
doing it.

The United Methodist Church cannot please the Triune
God—Creator, Son, and Holy Spirit—by retreating from the
inclusion of all people. This includes homosexuals who are
human beings with all the strengths and weaknesses of the
human species. God, in an amazing way, needs us all. There is
enough love for everyone. Why must we limit the "Wideness of
God's Mercy" to our own narrow prescriptions, definitions,
and agendas? Our writers remind us that, as the Body of Christ,
the Church must hold together, acknowledging differences,
celebrating diversity, and using our minds and hearts to prayerfully discern God's will for us in these crucial times.

Introduction

Tex Sample

The Loyal Opposition

The United Methodist Church is embroiled in controversy over the issue of homosexuality. In spite of a deep division in the denomination, a diminishing majority of delegation members at the General Conference continue to hold to the position that the practice of homosexuality is incompatible with Christian teaching. We believe that a majority would have already voted down this official position were the moderates in the Church not afraid of the impact of such a change on the denomination. The result of such a situation is that many United Methodists, like those who write for this volume, find themselves conscience stricken over the denomination's stand. To disagree so thoroughly with the Church that bore you, that you care for profoundly, that has been central to your faith and to your love of Christ, provokes a crisis not quite like any other in one's life.

Indeed, the very Church that nurtured us is the compelling reason to open the heart of the community of faith to the devoted United Methodist gay and lesbian people we know. We want to open the doors of the Church because of what we have been taught by that very Church. Every writer in this volume looks back to the inspiration we found in congregations, in the witness of laity and clergy, and in the work of the larger church.

We cannot understand our lives apart from this tradition. Such experience only makes the current impasse more painful.

No contradiction runs deeper than one that divides us at the point of the ultimate convictions of our lives. We cannot oppose the Church apart from our loyalty to it; we cannot be loyal without opposing it. We are caught in such a contradiction, but there is no glee here about such caughtness. So we struggle in these pages with how to be loyal to the Church we love and to oppose it on a stand where we thoroughly believe it is wrong.

Therefore, the work here is one of resistance. It is a time for those in the denomination who are deeply loyal to The United Methodist Church, but who reject its stand on homosexuality, to move more actively into resistance to its official policy on this issue. There is more than one way to resist, and we believe that anyone who sees this official position as a violation of conscience and the gospel can find faithful means to resist. Resistance is a Christian virtue. As long as the principalities and powers of the world remain in distorted and twisted violation of their destiny in God, Christians will find it necessary to resist. Indeed, resistance is basic to the church's life in withstanding the kind of cultural accommodation that violates the gospel and in opposing attempts to victimize people who live on the margins of a society.

A sizable literature now exists on resistance. It provides a useful tool for United Methodists who seek next steps in this turbulent time. A number of types of resistance fit the circumstances of our situation in The United Methodist Church. The work in this volume provides resources for each of these types.

Political Resistance and Everyday Resistance

It is important in addressing homosexuality to make a distinction between political resistance and everyday resistance.[1] By political resistance we mean overt and active acts at the local, district, annual conference, jurisdictional, and General Conference levels. Legislative proposals and lobbying efforts such as those by Affirmation, Reconciling Congregations, the United Methodist Federation for Social Action, and others are

examples of this. Pastors who engage in ecclesial disobedience
are also clear examples of political resistance. Such efforts must
continue. Presently, it does not appear that the vote of General
Conference will change in the near future, and such efforts to
keep the issue before the Church and to make progress toward
an official change require these kinds of efforts.

Yet, for many United Methodists, everyday resistance is a
more realistic direction. Many are not in situations where they
have sufficient numbers of others to work with, and some are
too personally vulnerable to take on such actions. We think
here, for example, of gay and lesbian people who could be
outed without their permission or otherwise placed in even
more untenable positions. Also, many people—especially those
who have not had much experience in this work—may not be
ready to take more overt action, at least to begin with.

Everyday resistance takes place in a thousand different ways.
It is refusing to laugh at heterosexist jokes, countering comments in conversations, challenging "biblical interpretations"
that characterize all same-sex acts as sinful and idolatrous, and
it is contradicting claims that homosexuals can be "changed"
from their orientation. It is forming friendships among gay, lesbian, and straight people, setting up connections among con-
crete lived people whose relationships fly in the face of
stereotypical images and prejudicial views. Everyday resistance
is protecting a person who chooses not to come out because she
or he holds a denominational office or pastorate, or some other
post in the Church. Everyday resistance happens at times and
places often hardly noticed beyond the moment of its occur-
rence.

I remember a party in which one man had the attention of a
half dozen people. He told one joke after another, each one a
demeaning and stereotypical characterization of "butch dikes"
and "prissy queers." The bubble of atmosphere around the
group became a suffocating and oppressive ethos of heterosexism. The lived lives of gay and lesbian people became obscured,
disfigured, and violated in the "humor" of the jokester. Only
one person was not laughing. She finally said, "Some of my best
friends are homophobic and heterosexist, but you are not one

of them!" With that the laughter stopped, the bubble of atmosphere burst, and the members of the group began a litany of comments to the effect that they have "nothing against homosexual people." Everyday resistance is crucial not only because it can challenge such situations across a range of events in day-to-day life, but also because it offers first steps for those who want to contribute to change but need to begin somewhere less threatening than more overt action.

Places and Spaces

Everyday resistance also involves what Michel de Certeau describes as setting up "spaces" in the midst of the "places" of the powerful.[2] That is, the powerful build places where they control and sanction behavior, but the powerless, and those who live outside that status quo, set up spaces in the midst of the dominant order and live a different way of life there. We mean, for example, the lesbian couple who are schoolteachers and loyal members of a local church live their lives being faithful to one another, to their professions, and to their local church. They live out a life other than that around them. A local congregation becomes a space of welcome to gay and lesbian people and a community where gay, lesbian, and straight people find ways to be the church together. A denominational executive opens doors to gay and lesbian people and takes stands continually against heterosexist practices in the purview of that office. Or a local church member becomes the most informed person in that congregation on the issue and steadfastly counters interpretations of the Bible, faith, and life together that marginalize homosexual persons. These are but a few of the kinds of resistance found in everyday life.

To Refuse the Official World and "Official Truth"

Mikhail Bakhtin's study of Rabelais's writing on working people in the Middle Ages opens another range of practices of resistance.[3] He observes that these folk resisted the dominant order through festive and carnivalesque forms. In their resistance they used mockery, travesty, derision, debasement, abuse, and obscenities, and what Bakhtin calls the "rites of laughter." These marginal medieval people would also congregate on side streets, and to protest the king they would hold "uncrownings"—a form of what we might today call guerrilla theater—a dangerous act in their time. It was, reports Bakhtin, a utopia "enacted without footlights." No doubt a good many of these are not right for people of faith to use against others, but Bakhtin also describes their resistance to "the official world" and to "official truth." In their resistance they expressed criticism in festive form and conveyed their "deep distrust of official truth" and the official world (p. 269). Indeed, theirs was a rejection of the official world and an attempt to make "a complete exit from the present order of this life" (p. 274).

This refusal of the official teaching of The United Methodist Church on homosexuality is a basic direction needed for the immediate future. Such refusal will take on its strongest expression as it is done at grassroots levels throughout the Church. It is not necessary for such refusal to take angry, hostile forms, though in some cases it may. What we really need are voices from all across the Church talking honestly and sincerely about the devastation that official stands such as ours have done to homosexual persons. As these voices mount, there is really little that can be done to silence them. We must break the confidence of conservatives and some moderates that there is a broad consensus supporting the official position of the church. Such witness alone will enable others to speak more openly against our official stand.

Living the Truth

Vaclav Havel, the great Czech nationalist, addresses yet another form of resistance in what he calls "living the truth."[4] According to his view, truth is a weapon, and living the truth opposes the living of the lie. Hosts of people all over The United Methodist Church counter the official stand of the denomination and live out lives in protest of the notion that "the practice of homosexuality is incompatible with Christian teaching." Think of an ordinand in a conference who refuses to answer the questions of his Board of Ordained Ministry in the "proper way" and risks his future in the ordained ministry of The United Methodist Church. Think of a layperson in a hostile and reactionary situation continuing to speak against unbeatable odds and doing so in such an articulate way that his or her opponents can only make vague threats of impending doom to the denomination in the face of his or her thoughtful and more considered claims. Think of a band of clergy and laity who, as a very small minority, face up to withering opposition in their district and annual conference while refusing to be silenced. They are outvoted every time and often shouted down or ruled out of order, but their courage and commitment wear on those whose positions are more opportunistic and self-serving. Living the truth corrodes illusion. Meanwhile our scholars continue their work with tradition and scripture and the theological commitments of the Church. It is clear that this struggle is being won and that the preponderance of scholarly opinion now no longer supports the official position of The United Methodist Church. Perhaps even more importantly, faithful Christians, heterosexual and homosexual, form countless friendships all across this country, and their lived lives of love and care for one another bespeak an embodiment of the truth that far outdistances the capacity of any General Conference disposition to the contrary.

Resistance as World Making

Resistance is also a form of world making. Genovese, in his significant work on "the world the slaves made," reports on the capacity of African American slaves to build a sacred universe even in the midst of slavery.[5] While they were not able to fight against slavery per se, the slaves were able to cope more effectively with economic hardship and to counter the slave owners' depiction of their characters. The slaves developed practices of a sacred world in which they described and evaluated themselves in ways that stood against slave-owner ideology. They developed slave songs, slave religion, black preaching, and the black church as alternatives to that oppressive world. Unable to destroy slavery they nevertheless were able to create a space—in de Certeau's terms—that kept legal slavery from becoming spiritual bondage.

Such world making is profoundly afoot by gay, lesbian, and straight people throughout The United Methodist Church. It resists the deadly, numbing effects of an atmospheric exclusion. It challenges the defacing of committed relationships of gay and lesbian people. It renames people as Christian who have lived their lives in a language world of violative definition and character assault. And yet, we think of the growing number of congregations across The United Methodist Church that are places where the practices of worship, of preaching, of study, of small group life, and of discipleship are actively engaged in the making of another world. These congregations do not merely have a different perspective; they are, rather, places of life together. They are engaged in the construction of a world. While they would be the first to confess all the ways they fall short of the reign of God, these congregations are also the places where the new forms of life are being hammered out in the day-to-day living of the community of faith.

Certainly these forms of resistance do not exhaust the possibilities, but they do represent something of the direction available to a loyal opposition that cannot sit still. Obviously, we want to do more than resist, we want to change The United Methodist Church on this issue, and we want to influence the direction of the larger culture. We believe that the articles that follow offer not only important resources for resistance but provide rationale for a broader social change. An overview of what follows will suggest what is herein.

An Overview

Amy DeLong opens with a ringing call to action by those convicted of the need to change our Church's official position. Her passion and challenge set the stage for what is to come. Victor Paul Furnish follows with a discussion of the biblical references and allusions to same-sex practices that are used to support the official stand of The United Methodist Church. His work is a significant challenge to such readings of Scripture. In the next chapter Bishop Roy I. Sano turns to yet other texts in Scripture that offer quite a different response from the official one. This is an approach to Scripture not often pursued, and one that offers quite a different use of Scripture on this issue.

With fruitful effect Dwight W. Vogel examines the quadrilateral to consider its contribution to a reconsideration of the Church's official position. E. Dale Dunlap turns to the *Discipline* and the Social Principles to critique their use by the Church on homosexuality. His suggestions will be quite helpful in opposing the current employment of the *Discipline* and the Social Principles to prop up the official position. Meanwhile, L. Edward Phillips compares the difference in the way the Church approaches war and the way it approaches homosexuality. It is an important way to call into question the current official hysteria and its distortion of the Church's more traditional approach to such conflictual issues.

Gilbert Haven Caldwell, speaking from his long history in the Civil Rights movement, wonders where all those who struggled in that effort are now on the issue of homosexuality. His is a call to the silent to regain their voices on this crucial issue.

The next articles address resistance in the church quite directly in terms of the lived lives of the writers. Jeanne Audrey Powers, a longtime ecumenical executive in the Church, reports her lifetime of resistance and becomes a pattern for many now facing circumstances not altogether unlike hers. Barbara Troxell speaks from a seminary context in describing a life defending gay and lesbian persons and working to keep doors open in theological education. Susan Laurie's sermon is an autobiographical account of resisting the Church's efforts to make her—as a lesbian—invisible in the faith. It is poignant testimony. Terry Norman recounts his life as a husband with children and a United Methodist pastor. His account takes us through his difficult journey to authentic life as a gay man who now counsels other men in similar circumstances.

The issue of ecclesial disobedience looms large in the Church today. Ignacio Castuera opens this section with a call to such dissenters as representatives of doctrinal faithfulness. Joretta Marshall defends ecclesial disobedience as a spiritual discipline, and J. Philip Wogaman makes the case for ecclesial disobedience in cases where vulnerable people's lives are at stake.

In every case except one, the writers for this volume are active members of The United Methodist Church. The exception is John Kruse, who, after a long career as a United Methodist minister, is leaving the denomination. His reasons for doing so need to be heard across the Church. The concluding statement by Amy DeLong then brings the work to a close.

We believe these writers provide resources for the loyal opposition of the Church. It is our hope that their offerings of avenues of resistance and their lives as embodied resistance will contribute to the change so desperately needed in the official stand of The United Methodist Church on homosexuality.

Notes

1. See John Fiske's distinction between social and semiotic resistance in his *Television Culture: Popular Pleasures and Politics* (London: Routledge, 1988), p. 316. See also his *Understanding Popular Culture* (London: Unwin Hyman, 1989), pp. 20-21.

2. Michel de Certeau, *The Practice of Everyday Life,* trans. Steven F. Rendell (Berkeley: University of California Press, 1984), pp. 37-41.

3. Mikhail Bakhtin, *Rabelais and His World,* trans. Helene Iswolsky (Bloomington: Indiana University Press, 1984), pp. 196-277.

4. Vaclav Havel, *Living the Truth,* trans. Jan Vladislav (New York: Faber and Faber, 1990).

5. Eugene D. Genovese, *Roll, Jordan, Roll: The World the Slaves Made* (New York: Random House, 1976).

One of These Days   *Amy E. DeLong*

On Friday night, May 30, 1997, I knelt in front of my bishop as she laid hands on me and ordained me. That was a good day. I was hope-filled and optimistic as I stood at the threshold of my professional ministry. I had felt for years as if I were ready to take flight, and on that night, in that moment, I was soaring. I was ready to begin serving The United Methodist Church—my church—the church I love and believe in and trust.

So it is with great sadness that now, only two years after ordination, I find myself disappointed in and distrustful of our Church. I am weary and brokenhearted and angry. My heart is broken because I have come to understand that "my church" is a church sick with disease. The diseases of heterosexism, hatred, and prejudice have been allowed to take hold and grow deep roots in our denomination and in so many of our local churches.

I am angry at this Church because it legitimizes homophobia and discrimination. I am angry that our children are being taught to fear and reject those who are not like them. I am angry that gay people are being taught to hate themselves. I am angry at the way the Bible is used as a weapon to condemn. The United Methodist Church's treatment of gay and lesbian Christians is nothing less than sinful.

Tangible Evil

When I was going through the examination process for ordination, members of the committee criticized me for not having
a well-developed understanding of evil. They were right. I did
not. I believed the goodness and love of God were stronger and
far more irresistible than evil. Although I still believe this, I must
admit in these few years of ordained ministry I have become
much better acquainted with evil and its power.

❑ I've seen "Christian" picketers with signs that say
   "Two gay rights: AIDS and Hell." Evil!

❑ I preached a sermon once about the need to be inclusive of all people, including gays and lesbians. After
   worship a parishioner said to me, "I think all those
   homos should be shot." Evil!

❑ During a seminary discussion about homosexuality, I
   watched as a dear lesbian friend of mine was targeted
   for exorcism by a fellow student who thought homosexuality was caused by a demon possession. The
   "exorcist," with arms extended, screamed, "In the
   name of Jesus Christ, Satan, come out of her!" Evil!

❑ The Church proclaims that for people to be "fully
   human" the good gift of their sexuality must be
   "acknowledged and affirmed by themselves, the church,
   and society" (*Book of Discipline,* Par. 65G). But at the
   same time it continually "dis-integrates" gays and lesbians by withholding this acknowledgment and affirmation, saying the practice of homosexuality is "incompatible
   with Christian teaching" (Par. 65G). "Ceremonies that
   celebrate homosexual unions shall not be conducted by
   our ministers and shall not be conducted in our churches" (Par. 65C). "Self-avowed practicing homosexuals are
   not to be accepted as candidates, ordained as ministers,
   or appointed to serve in The United Methodist Church"
   (Par. 304.3). The Church refuses to offer gay and lesbian
   Christians the affirmation needed to feel fully human,
   and it forces many of them to suppress, deny, or hide
   their God-given sexuality. Evil!

I am aware that "evil" is an extremely strong word and it has taken me a while to use it. But using it has helped me name in startling terms what I understand to be ungodly and spirit-destroying. The cruel, hurtful words and actions that so many of us witness truly need to be so named. They need also to be recognized, not as insignificant, isolated incidents from ignorant people, but as the birth child of our Church's antigay rhetoric.

One of the first things I did after ordination was go to our conference office and pick up a bumper sticker which bore the rainbow stripes of the gay pride flag and the words, "The United Methodist Church: A Hate-Free Zone." I wanted that statement to be true, and so, with a combination of hope and idealism, I put the bumper sticker on my vehicle; but I took it off in less than a year because it is not true. We do not provide a "hate-free zone" to our gay and lesbian brothers and sisters. We provide a zone of ambiguity and fear and silence. I took it off because I didn't want gays and lesbians in search of a church home to think they could walk safely into any United Methodist church and be accepted fully and completely for who they are. The bumper sticker was a lie—too many of our churches are dangerous places for gay people.

The Church, in its official position and in its most recent rulings, has given the message that it has little interest in providing a "hate-free zone." It has little desire to serve our gay and lesbian brothers and sisters equally, lovingly, or compassionately. The language of this denomination has moved amazingly quickly from social justice, peace, and love to official complaints, chargeable offenses, laws, and trials.

We have become the Pharisees of old—judging, condemning, limiting, silencing those who believe that our position on homosexuality is damaging and life-destroying, and ultimately does not reflect the "kin-dom" of God. With every General Conference and Judicial Council ruling; with every trial; with every hateful word; with every unholy choice we are required to make I hear our people, gay and straight, lamenting, "What are we going to do with this Church?"

Privileging the Status Quo and Punishing the Vulnerable

At my 1998 annual conference a motion was presented and passed that we "defer voting on resolutions relating to sexual orientation for the remainder of the 1998 Annual Conference." As a conference we were to engage, for a year, in "dialogue" and "education" for the sake of healing. Although this resolution seems benign (who can argue with dialogue and education) and even wise, given the volatility of the issue and the level of our discourse, it was in fact quite harmful. We had the chance to make a statement about inclusiveness and justice, but instead we voted to wait a year and "heal." In this year of "healing," the gay and lesbian people who have been excluded from the church remained excluded for yet another year. While we "healed," Matthew Shepard, a young, gay student in Laramie, Wyoming, was tied to a fence post and pistol whipped to death. While we "healed," Billy Jack Gaither, a gay man in Alabama, died after he was beaten with an ax handle and set on fire. While we "healed," the Reverend Greg Dell, a distinguished pastor in Chicago, was brought to church trial and was suspended from pastoral ministry for one year because he felt called to extend the love and blessing of Christ to two gay men who wanted to share their lives in a committed relationship.

No one "healed" this year except the privileged insiders who are just tired of talking about all this—they got a year off.

It is disingenuous to imply that we all just need to stay at the table and continue to talk. The truth is, some have never sat at the table because they've been consistently excluded. So many gay and lesbian Christians have been denied access or have been silenced by fear of violence and recrimination. Dialogue—real, honest, truthful dialogue—is nearly impossible in The United Methodist Church. You cannot have a two-way conversation when one side is unrepresented or underrepresented. And as long as so many are mistreated, we cannot begin to heal.

They have treated the wound of my people carelessly, saying, "Peace, peace," when there is no peace. (Jer. 6:14)

Disposing and Dispersing the Faithful

On March 25 and 26, 1999, I sat in the sanctuary turned court-room (strangely indicative of the trend in our denomination from compassionate ministry to mercilessly enforced legalism) as Greg Dell was tried for "Disobedience to the Order and Discipline of the United Methodist Church." At one point during the trial, the lead prosecutor asked Greg why he simply did not leave The United Methodist Church for another denomination that permits gay unions. Greg responded, "This is my family. . . . I don't leave my family just because we're in disagreement." Unfortunately, Greg has learned the painful lesson that gay and lesbian folks know all too well, and that is no matter how much you may want to stay within the family, sometimes your family kicks you out.

Greg stated at the press conference, which was held after the guilty verdict and the punishment had been delivered, that he is just the latest in a long line of people who have been banished because of the Church's antigay policy. He is right. Far too many have left or have been quietly escorted out without causing a ripple. Their departures were not public affairs—the lights weren't on, the news reporters weren't there, the cameras weren't rolling. They are just gone, and our denomination has suffered immeasurably by the silence their absence has created and by the loss of their creativity, energy, and faithfulness.

During the trial, before the presiding bishop read the verdict, he made a statement in which he encouraged those of us observing not to let our response to the verdict "rent the Body of Christ." Although I had sensed throughout the trial that the bishop was a "friend" in this matter, his statement was still hurtful.[1] What he and so many others seem unwilling to acknowledge is that the Church is already rent. It was splintered long ago by our unconscionable treatment of these brothers and sisters—and it will continue to be as long as we discount their experiences and ignore their presence and dismiss their absence.

> The word of the LORD came to me: Mortal, prophesy against the shepherds of Israel: prophesy, and say to them—to the shepherds: Thus says the Lord GOD: Ah, you shepherds of Israel who have been feeding yourselves! Should not shepherds feed the sheep? . . . You have not strengthened the weak, you have not healed the sick, you have not bound up the injured, you have not

brought back the strayed, you have not sought the lost, but with force and harshness you have ruled them. So they were scattered, because there was no shepherd; and scattered, they became food for all the wild animals. (Ezek. 34:1-5)

I grieve for this Church and the way we have abandoned and scattered our gay and lesbian brothers and sisters.

The Heart of the Gospel

These stories of injustice, violence, and heterosexual privilege are not just my stories. They are the Church's stories. And there are many more to tell. This is the context of The United Methodist Church. And it is within this context that many of us are struggling to remain loyal while still engaging in acts of resistance and disobedience in order to bring about change.

The inclusion of gays and lesbians into the full covenantal life of the Church is not a peripheral issue. It is not a diversion from the real needs of the Church. It is at the heart of the gospel of Jesus Christ. We are to be about the business of mercy and love and justice; of breaking down, not building up, the restrictive walls which divide us; of extending God's acceptance and blessing to all people. How we treat the scattered, the marginalized, the stranger; how we treat those who don't have the luxury of waiting another year; how we treat those who don't have the privilege of being welcome at the table determines whether or not we have lived faithfully the gospel message of love.

I am reminded of these words, which come from an African American spiritual: "I'm gonna come to the welcome table. I'm gonna shout my troubles over. I'm gonna walk and talk with Jesus. I'm gonna tell him how you treat me, one of these days." One of these days is today. Our gay and lesbian friends are walkin' and talkin' with Jesus. And they are telling him how we're treating them.

May God give us the courage to lift our voices in prophetic witness, open our hearts, and let our brothers and sisters come to the welcome table—it is the gospel.

Note
1. For more information regarding Bishop Tuell's response to the Greg Dell trial, please see Appendix C.

HOMOSEXUALITY, RESISTANCE, AND SCRIPTURE

Chapter 1   *Victor Paul Furnish*

"The Loyal Opposition" and Scripture

Is it possible to dissent from the statement that "the practice of homosexuality is incompatible with Christian teaching" and still be faithful to the witness of Scripture? For those who assume that the Bible spells out God's will for all times and that it unambiguously declares homosexuality to be a sin, the answer is clearly No. They will conclude that in this particular matter a *"loyal* opposition" is out of the question, because an absolute biblical truth is at stake.[1] However, the presuppositions on which this conclusion rests cannot be allowed—or at the very least, must be regarded as seriously flawed. Enter, the loyal opposition!

First, the claim that the Bible spells out God's will once and for all contradicts Scripture itself, which attests that because God's claim is as boundless as God's grace, it can never be reduced to a static set of rules, laws, or teachings. Scripture calls God's people to the *never-ending* task of discerning what it means to be faithful within the varied and ever-changing circumstances of their life in the world. What is most distinctive about the Bible, and what accounts for its scriptural status within the church, is not what it reports or reflects about the specific moral judgments and decisions reached by our ancestors in the faith. What is most definitive and distinctive, as well as pervasive of Scripture, is the affirmation of One God who belongs to no other, and to whom all else belongs; and the attendant conviction that human flourishing—male and female—is utterly and continually dependent upon God's grace and faithfulness.

Second, to search the Scripture for judgments about homosexuality is to look for biblical answers to questions that were not and could not have been raised by the biblical writers themselves. Homosexuality, as we have come to understand it and to use the word, is not a biblical topic. There are a few passages that refer or allude to sex between males, and one that refers to sex between females. But these passages have nothing to say about "homosexual orientation," of which the ancient world had no notion, and for which, therefore, it had no equivalent expression.

No doubt, there is room for honest differences of opinion about the theological and exegetical issues that are involved here. It is, therefore, all the more important that the church resist the temptation to claim the status of "absolute biblical truth" for any of its own judgments—which are no less operative even when proof texts are being quoted. This means that no judgment the church makes about homosexuality should be exempt from review, revision, or repeal. Any such judgment must be assessed and constantly reassessed with respect to a twofold criterion: Is it an appropriate expression of *the gospel* from which we live and to which we are committed? And is it *credible* (this is not the same as being "acceptable"), given what is known about sexual orientation and the formation of sexual identity? If the church's witness is not thoroughly credible, it will not be relevant; and if it is not appropriate to the gospel, it will not be Christian. For our dialogue about what is appropriate to the gospel, the witness of Scripture is indispensable. But if we rely only on "what the Bible says" for our understanding of human sexuality, our judgments about homosexuality are bound to fail the test of credibility, no matter how insistently we may proclaim them. In what follows I will comment further on several of these matters, and then suggest why, in particular, the statement that homosexual practice is "incompatible with Christian teaching" should not be regarded as an incontrovertible "biblical truth."

I

To begin with, three basic points must claim our attention.

1. Scripture alone affords us access to the gospel, from which our understanding of what constitutes an appropriately Christian witness must derive. I have sought to phrase this carefully, because a great deal depends on our understanding of how the Bible functions as Scripture for the church. The writings that constitute the Old and New Testaments document, respectively, the faith and witness of ancient Israel and of the earliest Christian community. It is specifically through the writings of the New Testament that we can be in touch, by means of critical investigation and analysis, with the apostolic witness to the gospel. It is from this gospel, recovered from Scripture but not identical with it, that the believing community derives its self-understanding as the Body of Christ and its understanding of what is appropriately Christian.

2. The apostolic witness to the gospel is the affirmation that God's grace is revealed and bestowed in Christ as both an unconditional gift and an unconditional claim. It is this grace of God, which always finds expression in a believing community, that is the defining reality of all Christian faith and witness. This means that the Christian ethic is not given with the law; nor is it presented as some particular set of "moral standards" or displayed in some specific pattern of conduct. Rather, the Christian ethic is founded on the transforming reality of God's gracious, saving love, as that is revealed in Christ and experienced by those who allow it to reclaim, renew, and revitalize their lives again and again.[2]

But if this is so, what about the specific moral rules and teachings of the Bible? Do they not spell out the will of God? Do they not show us, quite concretely, what it means to live a Christian life? And are they not unanimous in condemning same-sex practices? These questions lead us to a third point, and require that we consider the two biblical passages most often cited as proof that homosexuality is "incompatible with Christian teaching."

3. On the one hand, the specific moral rules and teachings of

Scripture document the concern of the ancient Israelites and the first Christians to conform their lives, both corporately and individually, to their experience of God's grace and claim. But on the other hand, every one of the specific moral rules and teachings of Scripture is time bound and culturally conditioned. All of them presuppose certain beliefs about the physical world, human beings, and social relationships that we can no longer presuppose, or even that we know to be in error.

This is especially true of what the various biblical traditions and writers presuppose and say about gender, sex, sexual activity, and sexual relationships. Their moral rules and teachings on these matters were profoundly conditioned, for example, by the patriarchalism that pervaded ancient society; by that society's stereotyping of gender roles; by its complete lack of knowledge of the female reproductive system; and by its total ignorance concerning the complexities of sexual identity and sexual orientation. This need not surprise us, for how could it have been otherwise? And it need not dismay us, either, because what was most distinctive about the faith communities from which our biblical writings emerged was not their moral codes and teachings. What defined and distinguished their existence and commitments was their understanding of God, along with their self-understanding as people who were living out of God's grace.

The time-bound, culture-conditioned character of what the biblical writers presuppose and say about sex is well illustrated by the two passages often cited as the best evidence that Scripture condemns homosexual practices.[3]

In the so-called "Holiness Code" of Leviticus 17–26, there are two formulations of a rule prohibiting a male from having sex with another male (18:22 and 20:13). The code in which they stand is actually a compilation of regulations from various places and times, and of various kinds. Some are ethical imperatives (e.g., "love your neighbor as yourself," Lev. 19:18), while others are rules concerning ritual purity. In the latter, *moral* purity is not an issue, but uncleanness and pollution in the literal, physical sense. Thus, a menstruating woman is declared to be temporarily unclean, and along with her any man with whom she may have had sex (Lev. 18:19; 20:18); and the emission of semen is said to render a man temporarily unclean, and along with him any woman with whom he may have had sex (Lev. 15:16-18). Similarly, because pollution was also thought to occur when classes of things are *mixed* (each being adulterated by the other), the Holiness Code forbids breeding an animal "with a different kind," sowing a field "with two kinds of seeds," and wearing any garment that is "made of two different materials" (Lev. 19:19).

It is against this cultural background that the prohibitions of Leviticus 18:22 and 20:13 must be understood.[4] They condemn sexual relationships between males because the passive partner is required—as the Hebrew literally says—to "lie the lyings of a woman," thereby defiling his maleness and rendering his partner unclean as well. No *moral* considerations are involved in this rule; nothing is said about what may be "good" or "just" or "loving," and even if one man has been raped by the other, the victim is regarded as no less unclean than his assailant. It should be clear that this Levitical rule can offer the church no help at all for thinking through the *moral* aspects of homosexuality, or for understanding how to be in ministry with and for homosexual people.

Romans 1:26-27 is especially critical, because it is the only place in the New Testament where there is as much as one full sentence about same-sex intercourse, and the only place in the Bible where both male and female relationships are in view.

> For this reason God gave them up to degrading passions, for just as their females exchanged natural intercourse for unnatural, so also the males, abandoning natural intercourse with females, were consumed with passion for one another, males committing shameless acts with males and receiving in their own persons the penalty required by their error. (NRSV, adapted)

In this part of Romans (1:18–3:20) Paul is not specifying what Christians should or should not do (his specific moral instructions and appeals are presented in chapters 12–15), but emphasizing that the whole of humankind has fallen short of the glory of God, and is in need of God's saving grace (see Rom. 3:22*b*-23, 24).

Paul's comment about people abandoning "natural inter-

course" is made with reference to Gentiles specifically, and is
but one of several illustrations he offers of how their refusal to
acknowledge the one true God (Rom. 1:21) plunges them into
every conceivable kind of vice. This ethnic stereotype prevailed
among Jews in Paul's day, and is also evident, for example, in
the Wisdom of Solomon (late first century B.C.E.), which Paul
and the early church regarded as scriptural. There, idolatry is
identified as the root of all "sexual immorality" (Wisd. 14:12,
Anchor; NRSV: "fornication"), including the "interchange of
sex roles" (Wisd .14:26, *Anchor*; NRSV: "sexual perversion")[5]
that was presumed to take place in same-sex intercourse.
Although Paul does not hesitate to describe the latter as "unnatural" and an expression of "degrading passions," he offers no
reasons for these judgments, apparently taking it for granted
that his readers will agree. Fortunately, there are numerous
sources from his day that show us what people did typically presuppose about "homosexuality," and these help us to understand why the apostle's judgment was so decisively negative.
Three common presuppositions deserve special attention.

First, anyone who engages in intercourse with a partner of the
same sex is willfully overriding his or her own "natural" desire for
the opposite sex. This presupposition is reflected in Paul's references to females who "*exchanged* natural intercourse for unnatural" and males who were "*abandoning* natural intercourse with
females" to have sex with males. To the apostle and his contem-
poraries, both Christian and non-Christian, talk of "sexual orientation" or the complexities involved in the formation of one's
"sexual identity" would have sounded like so much gibberish.

Second, all homoerotic acts are inherently lustful, an expression of sexual appetites so out of control that intercourse with
the opposite sex can no longer satisfy them (Paul: "degrading
passions"). Many moral philosophers in the apostle's day
viewed pederasty in this way. A pederast was an adult male who
sought sexual gratification from boys in their early teens ("pederasty" derives from the Greek words for "boy" and "eros").
Many of these young boys had been driven into prostitution by
reason of their poverty. One also reads of youthful male slaves
being forced to smooth their skin, groom and dress themselves

as women, and yield to the sexual advances of their male owners. But also when a homoerotic relationship was consensual, it could be viewed as no less the expression of inordinate and insatiable lust.

Third, homoerotic intercourse violates the laws of "nature" (Paul: "unnatural"), because those laws (it was supposed) decree that the male is always to assume the dominant, active role, and that the female's role is to be submissive and passive. The reasoning was that when two males have sex, the male's "naturally" dominant role is compromised, and that when two females have sex, the role of the male is usurped.[6]

To sum the matter up, this sentence in Romans contains nothing that is distinctively Christian. Any Hellenistic Jew could have written it, and so could any number of the moral philosophers contemporary with Paul, with but a change here and there. More important, none of the presuppositions reflected in Paul's statement can be allowed to stand unchallenged, given what the best of modern research is teaching us about human sexuality. In our day, any credible judgment about homosexuality must have a sounder basis than these ancient presuppositions provide. Biblical statements about nature and the universe afford a useful analogy. Insofar as they accord with the fundamental witness of Scripture, that creation is a gift of God and that we are called to be faithful stewards of all that God has given, they may and must be constantly affirmed. However, we would be irresponsible in our stewardship of creation were we to rely on them for *specific judgments* about the morality of, for example, strip-mining, clear-cutting the earth's rain forests, or colonizing other planets; for what was presupposed in antiquity, and therefore in Scripture, about the physical properties and processes of the universe is demonstrably wrong. Similarly, we may affirm the biblical statements about sex, insofar as they accord with the fundamental witness of Scripture that sex is part of God's good creation, for which we have continuing moral responsibility. But scriptural counsels about sex that are based on discredited presuppositions can be of no *specific* help as we consider what it means in actual practice to be faithful stewards of our God-given sexuality.

II

Returning now to the statement that "the practice of homosexuality is incompatible with Christian teaching," I should like to suggest that it is much *too broad* in its condemnation of all homosexual practice, and that it reflects a much *too narrow* conception of God's claim.

First, when we are led by ancient stereotypes to refer in an undifferentiated way to "the practice of homosexuality," we are making no allowance for the fact that persons of homosexual orientation express their homosexuality in different ways— some promiscuously or exploitatively, to be sure, but others in the context of monogamous, long-term, faithful relationships. Moreover, homosexual practice is not always an expression of a homosexual orientation, just as heterosexual practice is not always an expression of a heterosexual orientation. And one psychiatrist has identified other "varieties of homosexual expression" as the "developmental homoerotic activity" of preadolescents, the "pseudohomosexuality" that arises not from sexual desire but from other kinds of psychological or social needs, the "situational homosexuality" that sometimes takes place where people are isolated from the opposite sex (for example, in prisons), and the "ideological or political homosexuality" that is expressed, for example, by women "who see sex with a man as a capitulation to the enemy."[7] When the church's pronouncements take no account of these kinds of distinctions, relying instead on texts that presuppose what can no longer be presupposed, they must be judged to have failed the test of credibility, even if they are sent forth under the banner of "biblical truth."

Second, when the "incompatibility" statement assumes that "Christian teaching" is the norm by which the believing community is to be guided, it is reflecting a conception of moral responsibility that is far less comprehensive than the affirmations of Scripture about the unlimited scope of God's claim. Jesus does not say, "Come, follow my teachings," but "Come, receive the promise of the Reign of God, and *become my disciples*." And Paul does not summon us to "walk according to

Christian teaching." He challenges us to "walk worthily of *the gospel*," and in the love with which, in Christ, God has *already* graced and claimed our lives. Here is the one unchanging and absolute norm of Christian faith and witness: the boundless grace of God as that is disclosed and confirmed in the gospel of Christ. And the boundlessness of God's grace is matched by the boundlessness of God's claim, which is not simply that one adhere to "Christian teaching."

This means that what the church teaches always stands under the judgment of the gospel, and has to be constantly reconceived and reformulated to take account of ever new realities, deeper insights, and an enlarging vision. Like God's grace, God's claim is boundless because it embraces our *lives*, whole and entire, that they may be defined and shaped by God's grace and ever newly expressive of it. So when it comes to sexual conduct, or anything else, the appropriate question is not, "What is compatible with Christian teaching?" The appropriate question is always and repeatedly, "How can the grace of God disclosed in Christ, out of which we live, be *lived out* most fully and appropriately in this place and under these circumstances?" The church's role is not to legislate summary judgments about what is Christian conduct and what is not. It is called to be a community where the question of what constitutes Christian conduct is continually being explored, reviewed, and critiqued; a community of moral inquiry, dialogue, and discernment; a community that is attentive both to the leading of the Spirit and to the realities of its particular time and place.

In short, Scripture does not and, in the nature of the case, cannot be expected to offer timeless statements about God's will. Rather, it summons the church to be constantly searching out what God requires (for example, Rom. 12:2; Phil. 1:9-11), because the will of God, like God's love, "is broader than the measure of our mind."[8] Thus the judgment that homosexual practice is "incompatible with Christian teaching" should not be baptized as a "biblical truth," and those of us who believe there are good reasons for rejecting such a statement can rightly claim to be both faithful to Scripture and loyal to the church.

Notes

1. Such a position is described as follows in the document, "In Search of Unity," which emerged from the Dialogue on Theological Diversity within The United Methodist Church (Nashville, November 20-21, 1997; Dallas, February 19-20, 1998): "Those who oppose the admission of homosexuals to the Church's orders and rites believe that such a proposed practice is inconsistent with Christian teaching. They believe themselves to be either explicitly or implicitly forbidden by scripture or by the teaching of our Lord Jesus Christ as reliably witnessed in scripture to accept this practice. From their point of view, to accept or condone these practices would be to undermine the authority of scripture and of Christ. It would be to reject the healing authority of the Word of God, or of God's definitive revelation, or of scripture in the church" (Section III, B, 1, "Different Understandings of the Authority of Scripture and Divine Revelation").

2. Compare Willi Marxsen, *New Testament Foundations for Christian Ethics* (Minneapolis: Fortress Press, 1993), pp. 1-22, 310-12.

3. For more details and documentation, as well as comments on the other biblical passages regularly cited in discussions about homosexuality, see my essay, "The Bible and Homosexuality: Reading the Texts in Context," in *Homosexuality in the Church: Both Sides of the Debate*, ed. by Jeffrey S. Siker (Louisville: Westminster John Knox Press, 1994), pp. 18-35; also, Robert L. Brawley, ed., *Biblical Ethics & Homosexuality: Listening to Scripture* (Louisville: Westminster John Knox Press, 1996).

4. This point is also made by, for example, Tikva Frymer-Kensky, "Sex and Sexuality," in *The Anchor Bible Dictionary,* ed. by David Noel Freedman, et al. (New York: Doubleday, 1992), 5.1145-46.

5. For this translation see David Winston, *The Wisdom of Solomon* (Anchor Bible, 43; Garden City: Doubleday, 1979), pp. 269 and 280. The NRSV rendering is a paraphrase.

6. For extensive discussion and documentation of this ancient view, see Bernadette J. Brooten, *Love Between Women: Early Christian Responses to Female Homoeroticism* (Chicago: University of Chicago Press, 1996).

7. Ruth L. Fuller, "What Does Science Teach About Human Sexuality?" in *Caught in the Crossfire*, ed. by Sally B. Geis and Donald E. Messer (Nashville: Abingdon Press, 1994), pp. 80-81.

8. Frederick W. Faber, "There's a Wideness in God's Mercy," #121 in *The United Methodist Hymnal* (Nashville: The United Methodist Publishing House, 1989).

Chapter 2

Roy I. Sano

Unity with Integrity in God's Mission

Debate over homosexuality threatens to dismember the Body of Christ. The contentious conflict discredits the witness of the church. In order to promote unity among Christians so others will believe in Jesus Christ (John 17:21), I will explore the broader and deeper biblical and theological foundations for unity with integrity in the mission of the Triune God. As I proceed, I will uncover reasons to affirm insights in positions which are generally treated as mutually exclusive as well as uncover reasons to propose changes in those positions if we are to build unity.

Ethics Based on the Work of the Creator

Let me begin with the most explicit biblical prohibition of homosexual practices.[1]

❑ "You shall not lie with a male as with a woman; it is an abomination" (Lev. 18:22).
❑ "If a man lies with a male as with a woman, both of them have committed an abomination; they shall be put to death; their blood is upon them" (Lev. 20:13).

While the injunctions are clear, an issue immediately arises. Why do we disregard the dreadful death sentence for violators?[2] Since an overwhelming majority of us refuse to adhere to this command, there is in this fact a common point to begin our reflections regardless of our views on homosexuality. I will pursue a line of reflection that explains why we can and must disregard the prohibition and the punishment.

1. I can appreciate the foundations for prohibiting homosexual acts: We are expected to live our lives in accordance with the intentions of the Creator. Any act that trespasses the goodness in God's created order is therefore a sin. The biblical prohibition of a man lying with a man as with a woman assumes that God created male and female and said it was good. From this perspective, homosexual acts understandably violate this ordering of creation and are sinful. Therefore, there is wisdom in this approach in that we are expected to live out what God created us to be.

2. Goodness in one ordering of creation, however, does not exclude goodness in another ordering: There is always a temptation to overextend a valid insight, and thus turn it into an evil.[3] Take, for example, the biblical passage that states or assumes that God created males and females. If we assume that this insight excludes any other ordering, we overextend the truth and turn it into a falsehood.[4] An instructive analogy appears in God creating various ethnic identities and cultures.

When the Jews returned from their exile in a foreign country and an alien culture, they rightly sought to renew their distinct God-given identity. It made sense to retell their stories and restore their rituals, to rebuild the temple and restore the walls around Jerusalem. They went further. They excluded foreigners from the temple and directed the people to divorce their foreign wives (Neh. 13:27-31; Ezra 10:10-43). If God created Jews and Gentiles as distinct people (Gen. 10), mixing ethnic identities was viewed as a transgression of the goodness which God created.[5]

Fortunately, other people within Judaism felt God nudging them to be more open, hospitable, and gracious toward foreigners. The story of Ruth, the Moabite, for example, can be read as the providential care of God creating a different identity by mixing a Gentile into the genealogy of King David, the model of a Jew as a royal priesthood. None other than Jesus Christ, the Savior of the world, and the Sovereign of all sovereigns, had an ancestry which crossed or transgressed the ethnic boundaries which God had created.

In his ministry, Jesus came to his own Jewish people and worked within their culture. He also moved among the Gentiles, the symbol of another ethnicity, as well as the Samaritans, the symbol of a people's identity mixed ethnically, culturally, and religiously. Accepting Samaritans was particularly problematic to his people because Jesus worked with and through another ordering of the human family than the division into Jews and Gentiles.

In addition to the issue of ethnicity, the teaching of Jesus concerning gender recognized another identity (in Matt. 19:3-12). Jesus accepted the distinction between women and men and therefore of marriage between them. Within this framework, Jesus also supported Moses in allowing divorce because of "hardness of heart" in people. When the listeners protested that his teaching somehow seemed impossibly high, Jesus said, "Not everyone can accept this teaching, but only those to whom it is given. For there are eunuchs who have been so from birth, and there are eunuchs who have been made eunuchs by others, and there are eunuchs who have made themselves eunuchs for the sake of the kingdom of heaven" (Matt. 19:11b-12). Eunuchs represent another ordering of creation than the distinction between male and female. Given the three "causes" Jesus mentions, we need not assume all eunuchs are the same. Most important, we need to note that some are eunuchs "from birth." A fundamental point applies. Mosaic injunctions concerning marriage and divorce do not apply to this distinct body of persons.[6]

In the same fashion, the missionary efforts of the apostles reached persons of other ethnic identities and sexuality. The Holy Spirit sent Philip to bear witness to Samaritans, as well as to a eunuch (Acts 8:1-40). In both cases they believed in Jesus Christ and were anointed with the Holy Spirit without circumcision.

The biblical analogy of ethnic and gender differences suggests we at least keep open to the possibility that homosexuality is part of God's created order. Do any other sources of knowledge suggest that homosexuality is part of God's created order? A review of recent scientific research suggests a high degree of possibility.[7]

3. A growing consensus about the "creation" of homosexual orientation suggests another ordering of human sexuality: Our biblical forebears did not know about homosexual *orientation*. They were concerned about homosexual *acts*. They assumed that God created male and female and that heterosexual acts between man and woman were the only acceptable acts. This meant homosexual acts were therefore contrary to the "nature" of all persons and the ordering of creation as they knew it. Only in the late–nineteenth century did we develop the concept of a homosexual orientation.[8]

Earlier, researchers looked to three major "causes" in explaining homosexual orientation and behavior. They are reminiscent of the origins of eunuchs in the teaching of Jesus (Matt. 19:11*b*-12). Researchers turned to prenatal developments, to social interactions after birth, and to the choices of the person as the key factors.

The three explanations were frequently reduced to nature in the case of prenatal factors and to nurture when choices were involved in interactions after birth. Rather than insisting on either one as the single determinative cause, there is a growing recognition today across the board that both nature and nurture are very complex mixtures of factors.

Furthermore, nature and nurture interact with each other in any number of ways. At particularly formative moments, one may dominate with countless combination of factors over the other, and vice versa at another stage of development. We are therefore speaking in a loose way when we speak of nature and nurture as discreet factors.

Even if further research locates a single genetic "cause," there will probably be variations in the circumstances which are formative for certain persons and not for others. Ensuing research into the formation of a person's sexual orientation will very likely propose several kinds of trajectories, and the most knowledgeable among us will probably be reluctant to claim that any explanation applies to the total range of homosexual identities we have begun to recognize.[9]

Original sin and the fall are of course inevitably involved in all of the created order. What is being discovered, however, in the origin and development of homosexuality cannot automatically and exclusively be classified as sinful or evil anymore than we can speak of heterosexuality as being an unqualified good in all its manifestations.

Finally, there is already considerable agreement that it is very difficult and often impossible to change sexual orientation once it is established. Some therefore focus on altering behavior and work much less to change sexual orientation. When "reparative therapists" speak of altering orientation, they often carefully specify its origins and development which they seek to correct.[10] This approach therefore leaves room for other origins and development of homosexuality such as the ones suggested in these reflections.[11]

Proceeding along these lines, it is better to think that there are instances when human sexuality has been "created," and is, therefore, natural and normal for some persons in the sense we recognized with ethnic identities. When I highlight forces beyond the individual's choices such as in God creating by fiat in Genesis 1, I associate the outcome with clear distinction between male and female heterosexuality. When I highlight the creative process which combines divine providence and human choices, as in Genesis 2 and in the genealogies we examined, I allow for exceedingly complex elements from both "nature" and "nurture." The latter process allows for complex and highly variegated interactions and the creation of variations in sexual orientation. I therefore find what is possible from biblical and theological reflections is highly probable in many instances on the basis of recent scientific investigations.

4. If we, as a church, ask homosexual persons to become heterosexuals or prohibit them from living out their identity, we ask them to transgress the identity they are given and violate the principle we have affirmed: This line of reflection leads me to

say that homosexuality is in some cases a person's "natural" condition and a gift from God.[12] Acting out a homosexual orientation is therefore not "unnatural" or against the "nature" of that person (Rom. 1:26-27). Rather, they are acting out a God-given orientation.

I return to the wisdom which began this line of reflection. If we ask homosexual persons to change their orientation to a heterosexual one, or prohibit them from responsibly living out their homosexual identity as is expected from heterosexual persons, we are asking them to transgress their identity.

By pursuing biblical and theological reflections in relation to recent scientific investigation, I have uncovered one line of thinking to explain why we disregard the prohibition in specific instances. These reflections also explain why we must therefore disregard the injunction to execute violators of the prohibition in Leviticus 18:22 and 20:13.[13] If this approach is not convincing, we still have to explain why we disregard the prohibition and/or the punishment if we say we adhere to the Bible.

Ethics Based on Salvation in Jesus Christ

1. We choose on the basis of an "either/or" option: The work of Christ as Savior has several implications concerning our debates. We begin with the "either/or" option which the early church confronted—either to require circumcision from Gentile converts or not. As is familiar, they decided at a gathering in Jerusalem not to require circumcision of Gentiles (Acts 15:1-29). The choice was based primarily on the experience of the apostles. While their decision appeared to disregard the biblical injunction (Gen. 17:9-14), they were adhering to a deeper dimension of the biblical faith. God is one. The God who is Savior in Jesus Christ, does not violate what the God who is Source and Creator has brought into existence.[14] The decision of Christians at Jerusalem meant that however much the Gentiles were changed in their conversion, they will not be expected to become Jews before they became Christians. As Peter said at the gathering in Jerusalem, to ask Gentiles to be

someone they are not is "putting God to the test by placing on the neck of the disciples a yoke that neither our ancestors nor we have been able to bear" (Acts 15:10).

Because circumcision involves an alteration of the genitals, it symbolizes what is required of homosexual persons when we virtually ask them to become heterosexual persons before we fully accept them as Christians. If such persons are given their homosexual orientation as a gift, we therefore face an "either/or" option. Either we require an alteration (a "circumcision"), or not. Reasons have been offered not to require an alteration of sexual orientation. However, asking God to alter someone's sexual orientation is asking God as Savior in Jesus Christ to contradict the work of God the Source or Creator. It is asking God to act with a divided mind, or it is having two gods.

2. A "both/and" is in order: Advocating acceptance of homosexual orientation can, however, be overstated, just as we noted in reviewing the opposite viewpoint. Changes can occur in several ways. First, some persons who are in the midrange of the spectrum of sexual orientations I cited earlier could conceivably change the trajectory of their sexual orientation at a formative period. Second, some persons may have become homosexual in orientation and practice for unfortunate reasons. For some of these persons we should allow for a "circumcision," or a change in orientation and practice. It is as if the process rectifies what has gone wrong and enables those persons to become who God intended them to be. Third, it is also conceivable that some homosexual persons willingly choose not to practice their homosexuality without changing their orientation.

The choices made by the apostle Paul are instructive. In accord with the decision about the "either/or" option at the gathering in Jerusalem, Paul refused to allow Titus, a Gentile, to be circumcised (Gal. 2:3). And yet, when it came to Timothy, Paul allowed him to be circumcised, primarily because he was Jewish since his mother was a Jew (Acts 16:1-3). The fact that Paul refused to have Titus circumcised and allowed Timothy to be circumcised indicates that Paul followed what we can call a "both/and" approach.[15] The combination of the "either/or" and "both/and" approaches in Paul offers us an avenue of affirming insights in the positions which are regularly seen as contradictory. Furthermore, correctives have been suggested because the insights of both positions are only applicable to a range of persons.

3. Death and Resurrection in Christ are still expected: While we are called to affirm the diversity God has created, we still expect all of our identities and cultures to undergo death to sin and the evil ways expressed through those gifts. By going through death and resurrection with Jesus Christ, we rise to newness of life with Christ (Rom. 6:1-6). While advocates for acceptance of homosexuality could be more vocal on the point of ethical and moral growth among homosexual persons, the media coverage of the public debate over homosexuality could also report more fully the discussion along these lines.[16] Let me now turn to an outline of the graces and gifts which the Holy Spirit makes possible through the death and resurrection in Jesus Christ.

Ethics Based on Sanctification of the Holy Spirit

1. A "neither/nor" becomes necessary: Paul's struggle with his condition illustrates the work of the Holy Spirit in relation to our topic. Why Paul pleaded for a cure to his illness is perfectly understandable. The Bible says he is disqualified from leadership. "No descendant of Aaron the priest who has a blemish shall come near to offer the LORD's offerings by fire; since he has a blemish, he shall not come near to offer the food of his God" (Lev. 21:21).

Despite this exclusion, Paul reports:

> Three times I appealed to the Lord about this [limitation], that it would leave me, but he said to me, "My grace is sufficient for you, for power is made perfect in weakness." So, I will boast all the more gladly of my weaknesses, so that the power of Christ may dwell in me. Therefore I am content with weaknesses, insults, hardships, persecutions, and calamities for the sake of Christ; for whenever I am weak, then I am strong. (2 Cor. 12:8-10)

No physical change occurs, and yet there is a transformation of Paul's spirit by the grace of God. What Leviticus calls a "blemish" is not removed, but the power of Christ is made perfect at the point of Paul's "weakness." Many denominations have therefore reversed their exclusion of persons with handicapping conditions from clergy ranks despite the exclusion in Leviticus. Since the "blemishes" in Leviticus 21 include conditions which could have been given in birth, including "a limb too long, . . . a hunchback, or a dwarf" (21:18, 20), we apply this principle to homosexual persons to the extent that prenatal developments are often a major factor.

As we have seen in the work of God as Source in the Creator and as the Savior in the Christ, the work of God as Spirit does not alter a person's sexuality no matter how much it undergoes conversion from any abuse and exploitation. What becomes important is the transformation of the person with the graces and gifts of the Spirit. Therefore, beyond the "either/or" which led Paul to reject circumcision for Titus, and beyond the "both/and" which led him to circumcise Timothy, Paul employs a "neither/nor." Paul writes, "For in Christ Jesus neither circumcision nor uncircumcision count for anything; the only thing that counts is faith working through love" (Gal. 5:6). Again in Galatians, he says, "For neither circumcision nor uncircumcision is anything; but a new creation is everything!" (Gal. 6:15). Finally, to the Corinthians he writes, "Circumcision is nothing, and uncircumcision is nothing; but obeying the commandments of God is everything" (1 Cor. 7:19).[17]

2. The Holy Spirit nurtures graces and gifts: The Holy Spirit mediates the graces for the moral life and the gifts for ministries in God's mission. They basically apply equally to all of us regardless of our sexual orientation. We can only list them summarily in this setting.

Living in an ecology of grace made accessible by Jesus Christ means we will grow in grace. We will therefore "boast in our sufferings, knowing that suffering produces endurance, and endurance produces character, and character produces hope, and hope does not disappoint us, because God's love has been poured into our hearts through the Holy Spirit that has been

given to us" (Rom. 5:3-5. See too, for example, 2 Peter 1:5-11).
Paul expected Christians in Galatia to bear fruit (singular, as if
they go together) of the Spirit because of this growth in grace:
"love, joy, peace, patience, kindness, generosity, faithfulness,
gentleness, and self-control" (Gal. 5:22).[18]

I find several lists of the gifts of the Spirit for ministry in
God's mission. A sampling appears in Ephesians 4. Because of
the diversity of gifts, "some [are] apostles, some prophets, some
evangelists, some pastors and teachers." The immediate purpose is "to equip the saints for work of ministry." The gifts of
the Spirit enable believers to participate in the ministries of
Jesus Christ who sought to "fill all things," in the depth, the
breadth, and the heights, with the fullness of the God who is
"above all and through all and in all" (Eph. 4:1-16).[19]

There are additional consequences to the anointing of the Holy
Spirit for God's mission which we frequently overlook. The
anointing of the Holy Spirit empowered Jesus to address issues of
justice and liberation. Luke's use of the Servant Song in Isaiah
61:1-2 has become familiar. The Spirit anoints him "to bring
good news to the poor, to proclaim release to the captives and
recovery of sight to the blind, to let the oppressed go free"
because he brought the jubilee (Luke 4:18-19; Lev. 25:10).[20]
Justice as the means to these ends is highlighted in Matthew's use
of another Servant Song. The anointing enables Jesus to "proclaim justice to the Gentiles." Those in the struggle for justice
who are "bruised reeds" will not be broken, nor will the "smol-
dering wick" burning with a longing for God's reign be quenched,
until this servant "brings justice to victory" (Matt. 12:18-21,
from Isa. 42:1). We often miss these spiritual dimensions in the
struggles for justice and liberation. These efforts become simply
secular when Christians fail to participate with their graces and
gifts of the Spirit as Jesus and other biblical forebears did.

Conclusion

I have explored biblical and theological foundations to see
who the Triune God is and what this God says and does. By recognizing the distinct contributions of diverse viewpoints, as well

as their need for correctives, we are led to walk more humbly in faith. There are reasons to acknowledge instances of homosexuality which are part of God's created order, to promote salvation from sinful expression through death and resurrection in Jesus Christ, and to hallow the lives of all persons through the Holy Spirit with the graces of moral life and gifts for ministries in God's mission. Finally, amidst growth along these lines, we see why we can and must join the struggle for justice and liberation so that the fullness of God's reign and realm will come and the earth will be covered with the knowledge of the Lord Jesus Christ, just as the waters cover the sea (Isaiah 11:9). Dear God, help us. Amen.

Notes

1. I cannot debate the merits of the passages generally cited in support of the church's stand, except to note that some passages raise issues about interpretation (Gen. 19 and Judg. 19) and others of translation (1 Cor. 6:9 and 1 Tim. 1:10). It will become less important to debate these and other passages if the line of reflection offered here on the passages from Leviticus are cogent.

2. We consistently violate other prohibitions in Leviticus. For example, we are clearly told, "You shall not let your animals breed with a different kind; you shall not sow your field with two kinds of seed; nor shall you put on a garment made of two different materials" (Lev. 19:19). Despite these prohibitions we practice animal husbandry, cross-fertilize plants, and wear clothing which often mix in various ways cotton, wool, silk, and synthetics. Richard E. Whitaker offers good reasons for disregarding the prohibitions in his essay, "Creation and Human Sexuality," in *Homosexuality and Christian Community*, Choon-Leong Seow, ed. (Louisville: Westminster John Knox Press, 1996), pp. 3-13. See too, Patrick D. Miller, "What the Scriptures Principally Teach," in the same volume, especially, p. 62, n. 7 concerning John Calvin's view on different laws and commands in the Bible.

3. The call to stay within the boundaries God sets is often overlooked by its advocates. We often disobey God's will with an uncritical adherence to the letter of the law or a particular aspect of the total truth, as well as an unreflective zeal to demonstrate the promises of God. The source of the problem lies in overextending a valid insight. The serpent first tempts Eve with an exaggeration of God's word (Gen. 3:1-3), just as the devil tempts Jesus excessively to demonstrate God's goodness and power (Matt. 4:1-11; Luke 4:1-13).

4. See for example the role Romans 1:26-27 plays in *The Moral*

Vision of the New Testament: Community, Cross, New Creation by Richard B. Hays (San Francisco: HarperCollins, 1996), pp. 379-406.

5. According to Matthew 1:1-17, Ruth is only one of the four points where Gentiles were mixed into the genealogy of Jesus. In addition, Tamar and Rahab were also Gentiles by birth, as was Bathsheba, by marriage to Uriah, the Hittite.

6. The passage in 2 Timothy 3:16, "all scripture is inspired of God," it refers to the Hebrew Bible, including the wisdom literature. Choon-Leong Seow reminds us in his essay, "A Heterosexual Perspective," in *Homosexuality and Christian Community* that the wisdom tradition used reason to reflect critically on experiences (pp. 14-27). Since scientific investigation represents a highly developed method of reflecting on human experiences, we pay attention turn to developments in science.

7. This step in the line of reflection summarizes selected points discussed at length by Francis Mark Mondimore in his study, *A Natural History of Homosexuality* (Baltimore: Johns Hopkins University Press, 1996), pp. 97-193. After surveying a number of disciplines, Mondimore concludes, "Homosexuality is a natural, abiding, normal sexuality for some people. It is not a disease state, not simply a behavior, and not subject to change. It develops in some individuals as a result of influences of heredity, prenatal development, childhood experiences, and cultural milieu in varying combinations. No one influence seems either necessary or sufficient—homosexual orientation is a possible outcome in many different circumstances because the human mind is uniquely evolved to be rich in possibility" (p. 249; see also, pp. xii and 157).

8. The concept of homosexuality as an orientation beyond homosexual activities or practices was introduced into European thinking in 1869 through writers such as Karl Maria Kertbeny in Germany. See Mondimore, p. 3.

9. See Mondimore's summary of six categories on a spectrum from an exclusively heterosexual orientation to an exclusively homosexual orientation in *Sexual Behavior in the Human Male* by Alfred Kinsey, Wardell Pomeroy, and Clyde Martin (Philadelphia: W. B. Saunders, 1948), pp. 78-89.

10. To argue on the basis of sin or evil, such as the ratio of promiscuity, illnesses, and deaths among homosexuals in comparison to heterosexuals, is seriously flawed when it does not take into account the social and cultural contexts and the religious sanctions and political measures which enforce them.

11. Concerning "reparative therapy," see, for example, Joseph Nicolosi, "What Does Science Teach About Human Sexuality?" in *Caught in the Crossfire: Helping Christians Debate Homosexuality,* edited by Sally B. Geis and Donald E. Messer (Nashville: Abingdon Press, 1994), pp. 67-78. In the same volume, a different position

appears in Ruth L. Fuller, "What Does Science Teach About Human Sexuality?" (pp. 78-88).

12. An instructive history of the issues involved scientific research and political battles to change homosexuality from a disease to a variation on human sexuality appears in Ronald Bayer's, *Homosexuality and American Psychiatry: The Politics of Diagnosis* (Princeton, N.J.: Princeton University Press, 1987).

13. Bishop Melvin E. Wheatley says, "Homosexuality, quite like heterosexuality, is neither a virtue nor an accomplishment. It is a mysterious gift of God's grace communicated through an exceedingly complex set of chemical, biological, chromosomal, hormonal, environmental, developmental factors totally outside my homosexual friend's control. His or her homosexuality is a gift—neither a virtue nor a sin." Cited in Geis and Messer, p. 179.

14. Ulrich W. Mauser balances an ethic based on creation and an ethic based on salvation in his chapter on "Creation, Sexuality, and Homosexuality, Homosexuality and Christian Community," pp. 39-49, esp. p. 45. This presentation disagrees with Mauser, however, because he assumes the creation in Genesis 1 is the only way creation happens.

15. Requiring this choice or changes in orientation of all homosexual persons, is, however, to repeat Peter, "putting God to the test by placing on the neck of the disciples a yoke that neither our ancestors nor we have been able to bear" (Acts 15:10).

16. The "both/and" approach is also evident in Paul's treatment of specialties in ministries. First, Paul recognized his speciality in ministry among the uncircumcised and Peter's speciality among the circumcised (Gal. 2:7). Specialization did not, of course, exclude the alternative. That is, Paul often began his evangelism in synagogues among the Jews and Peter interacted with Gentiles. Second, Paul employed the both/and approach in his attempt to overcome the divisive party spirit in the church at Corinth. He named specialities in ministry and allowed for those specialities among himself, Apollos, and Peter (1 Cor. 1:12, 3:22), because they are all a part of God's mission (1 Cor. 3:6). This presentation proposes what is usually depicted as mutually exclusive options be seen as specialities in ministry within the total mission of the triune God.

17. In his speech cited earlier, Bishop Melvin E. Wheatley says, "Homosexuality is a gift—neither a virtue nor a sin. What she/he does with their homosexuality, however, is their personal, moral, and spiritual responsibility. Their behavior as a homosexual may therefore be very sinful—brutal, exploitative, selfish, promiscuous, superficial. Their behavior on the other hand, may be beautiful—tender, considerate, loyal, other-centered, profound." Cited in Geis and Messer, p. 179.

18. We find comparable characterizations of persons who live in the Spirit in 2 Cor. 6:1-10; 8:1-7; Eph. 4:1-10; Phil. 4:8-9; Col. 3:12-17; and 1 Thess. 4:1-8.

19. Other lists for the gifts of the Spirit also appear in Rom. 12:3-8; 1 Cor. 12:4-11, 27-31.

20. The anointing of a servant of God or Savior for liberation is not unique to the New Testament. We read in the book of Judges about the unpromising persons in unlikely moments becoming liberators from oppression after the children of Israel settled in the land of promise. They include Othniel (Judg. 3:10), Gideon (Judg. 6:34), Jephthah (Judg. 11:29), and Samson (Judg. 15:14).

Homosexuality, Resistance, and the Quadrilateral

Chapter 3 *Dwight W. Vogel*

Homosexuality and the Church

Evangelical Commitment and
Prophetic Responsibility

A Confessional Statement

My journey began in the sixties; it was slow, long, and painful. It involved wrestling with scripture, tradition, theology, and Christian experience through study, prayer, and the search for ongoing discernment. It was framed by my commitment to Jesus Christ as my Lord and Savior, and my response to God's call to proclaim the good news of Jesus Christ. I believe the theological matrix of my position is an "evangelical" perspective in the truest sense of that term: one based on the good news of Jesus Christ and inviting the response of faith through love and justice.

Scripture

I join my evangelical brothers and sisters in believing that scripture is the primary source for theology, though I do not believe that it is the only source. Scripture without interpretation and appropriation is dead. God's word to us is a living word, not a static reality. Rather, it is a dynamic empowered by the Holy Spirit through which we are addressed, challenged, opened to transformation, and enabled for faithful discipleship.

What does Scripture say about homosexuality? Since I am not a biblical scholar, I will not pretend to shed new light on the debate in this quarter. It is enough for me to know that there is in fact a scholarly debate about the answer to that question, and I turn instead to what is much more decisive for my theologizing; namely, hermeneutics (in this regard, the interpretation of Scripture).

The New Testament writers themselves are involved in the interpretive process. Questions concerning circumcision and dietary laws are raised, and the decisions made are articulated within what later becomes the canon. Their writings were not within the canon when first written, however. They point to the struggle of what the Christian community is to do with what was once accepted, but no longer fits the emerging life of faith. For us, these questions are not confined to appropriating the demands of the earlier testament. We face them when we have to decide what to do about the directive that "women should keep silence in the churches. For they are not permitted to speak, but should be subordinate" (1 Cor. 14:34), or that "a woman ought to have a veil on her head, because of the angels" (1 Cor. 11:10).

Such passages reflect the cultural conditioning of the age in which they were written. After study, we conclude that they do not reflect the deepest and most penetrating insights of the writer, and are not in keeping with the dominant thrust of New Testament witness. Such conclusions involve interpretation. Accepting such directives "literally" is also a matter of interpretation. That does not mean that one interpretation is just as good as another. It means that one must live into and out of the biblical witness in such a way that the Holy Spirit may grant us the gift of discernment. It is the challenge a pastor faces in every sermon: is there a "word from the Lord"? What is God saying to us today?

John Wesley's father told him that the best book for interpreting Scripture was the Bible itself. I have been working with some of the concerns and dynamics in Luke's writings. So I ask myself: what would be the response of the Jesus Luke portrays? And I confess that it would be very difficult for me to find the Jesus of Luke's Gospel (who goes out of his way to associate with and affirm women and outcasts and the ritually unclean of his day) judging homosexual behavior as in itself sinful.

The God Jesus reveals to us is not concerned with tithing "mint, and dill, and cummin" to the neglect of the weightier matters of the law: "justice and mercy and faith" (Matt. 23:23).

All too often it seems that we are straining out a gnat and swallowing a camel (Matt. 23:24). That is, when we should be concerned about the quality of relationship, with whether or not there is physical or mental abuse, with whether or not there is within the relationship that which builds each partner up or only tears one or both down, we are instead concerned about whether that relationship is heterosexual or homosexual.

Finally, scripture gives me revelation of a God who is not capricious, but seeks the very best for us. "Commandments" are for a purpose. In this context, the strain of New Testament teaching which addresses me is compassion, love, and wholeness empowered by the Holy Spirit. That is the nature of the discipleship to which God calls me through Scripture.

Tradition

For me, Tradition refers not to the traditions which churches, or even *the* church, has, but with the dominant thrust of the church's teaching. The church does not always understand what is central and what is tangential at any given time. There have been periods when the church has thought that the view that the earth revolved around the sun was heresy, or that there was an implicit approval of slavery within the Tradition. We have no qualms about saying the church was wrong in these regards, that it misunderstood the nature of its own Tradition.

We are called upon to discern (with the help of the Holy Spirit) what is central to the Tradition of the church and what is culturally conditioned baggage, which we have confused with that Tradition. I find in baptism and the celebration of the Lord's Supper affirmations by the church of the worth of all God's children and the call to love and justice inherent in them. I am called to help the church come to see that its Tradition has to do with covenant and commitment and love and compassion, much more than to whether the partner who is God's gift to me is male or female.

There is not only the Tradition of the church catholic, however, but also the tradition of the denomination of which one is a part. This is articulated for me in *The Book of Discipline of The United Methodist Church* in the sections under Doctrinal Standards and

Our Theological Task and Social Principles.[1] Within this larger
context, there are specific references to sexual orientation:

> We insist that all persons, regardless of age, gender, marital
> status, or sexual orientation, are entitled to have their human
> and civil rights ensured. . . . Homosexual persons no less than
> heterosexual persons are individuals of sacred worth. All persons
> need the ministry and guidance of the church in their struggles
> for human fulfillment, as well as the spiritual and emotional care
> of a fellowship that enables reconciling relationships with God,
> with others, and with self.[2]

The position I am taking is an attempt to articulate and incar-
nate in action these affirmations. However, the next sentence
reads: "Although we do not condone the practice of homosexuality and consider this practice incompatible with Christian
teaching, we affirm that God's grace is available to all."[3] Does
this mean that if I take the tradition of my denomination seriously, I must accept this sentence as well?

It is part of the Tradition of United Methodists to engage in
work that analyzes, critiques, and when appropriate, seeks to
change what the *Discipline* says. We are not willing to let a pope
or even the Council of Bishops make those pronouncements.
Rather they must be worked out by democratic process. One is
not unfaithful to the tradition when one engages in such activity. Indeed, the very living out of the tradition of conference
necessitates it. It is love for the Church and concern for the wel-
fare of the denomination which provides the context for living
out our calling to serve the Church as loving critics. To do less
is to refuse to take the tradition seriously, to not engage it, or to
live in isolation from it. That may be safer, but it is not responsible.

Reason

Theology proper seeks to articulate in comprehensible and
coherent ways the content of the faith. Since I am conditioned
by my education in systematic theology, it is natural for me to
think this through in terms of some of its categories:

The Nature of God

What is the nature of the God I worship? Early on, I determined that the nature of God as Love is basic, and that God's righteousness is manifested by a demand for justice and compassion, rather than ritual purity. What does this have to say about homosexuality?

The God in whom I believe is opposed to oppression. God desires all persons to be as fully themselves as they can be. God's demand for justice is that such persons not be the subject of discrimination or oppression. The God whose nature is love and justice brings judgment against hate and fear. This hate and fear causes some persons to condemn others who are trying to live out their discipleship through a relationship they believe God has given them. To focus on one area (whether as an individual, an institution, or a church), and make one's position on that one issue the defining characteristic of faithful discipleship is a kind of idolatry.

Wherever care and compassion characterize human relationships and help the persons involved to be whole and healthy persons, there I believe God is at work. I find it hard to believe that this kind of God would judge the quality of the relationship on the basis of whether they were of the same sex or of different sexes. The God in whom I believe would be at work maximizing intimate relationships to be sacraments of divine love.

In a personal conversation, Mother Teresa said to us: "Please pray that we may be faithful and not interfere with God's work." I suppose it is finally a question of whether we are being faithful or interfering with God's work. That depends on whether God is something like the concept of God I have or not. Why do I believe God is this kind of God? Because of Jesus.

Christology

I have already referred to the picture of Jesus painted by Luke, a Jesus concerned with compassion, including the outsider, judging those who wanted to judge others on the basis of external characteristics, refusing to be contained by the social expectations of his religious or cultural setting. Those are characteristics that are important to my understanding of Jesus Christ.

But my Christology involves more than this. In renewal of the baptismal covenant, I am asked: "Do you confess Jesus Christ as your Savior, put your whole trust in his grace, and promise to serve him as your Lord?" The saving work of Christ is sometimes focused exclusively on the cross. I believe his saving work includes incarnation, life and ministry, resurrection and coming consummation, as well as his death. Thus, the salvation which Christ offers includes both the forgiveness of personal sin, the work of reconciliation, and liberation from oppression.

A basic text for me in this regard has been Ephesians 2:13-16. Although the writer is dealing with the relationship between Jew and Gentile in the early church, the implications I find in this passage are much more wide reaching:

> But now in Christ Jesus you who once were far off have been brought near in the blood of Christ. For he is our peace, who has made us both one, and has broken down the dividing wall of hostility, by abolishing in his flesh the law of commandments and ordinances, that he might create in himself one . . . in place of the two, so making peace, and might reconcile us both to God in one body through the cross, thereby bringing the hostility to an end. (RSV)

Certainly there has been hostility expressed in this area of the church's life. Yet there is none without sin, and all are in need of grace. We often misunderstand the nature of our sin. I may focus on some aspect of outward behavior, only to be led by the Spirit to recognize its root at a deeper and more interior level. Sometimes lust, promiscuity, or certain kinds of sexual intimacy are spoken of as if they were present only in homosexual relations, and then a judgment is made on that basis about homosexuality in general, rather than dealing with what makes such activity sinful.

I believe that Christ calls us to be reconciled with God and with each other. An important part of this reconciliation is the recognition that what disrupts this peace, this wholeness in Christ, is not restricted by one's sexual orientation. Abuse, infidelity, lack of concern for the health of one's self or one's partner—these are sins whatever the orientation. The person and work of Jesus Christ call us to a ministry of reconciliation.

Ecclesiology

We share one baptism—male and female, heterosexual and homosexual, and a whole continuum of theological perspectives. God's grace is given to each of us, and the Holy Spirit empowers us with gifts for both our life together and our ministry in Christ's name. When we cut ourselves off from others to whom God's gifts and grace are given, we impoverish ourselves and restrict the expression of the one body we are called to be.

If we are "eager to maintain the unity of the Spirit in the bond of peace," there will be special challenges to our good intentions when we disagree with one another. There are particular dangers when we take it upon ourselves to describe an opposing position or the persons within it. What we say may become inflammatory, and when our observations are inaccurate as well, the response of those who feel attacked will likely be passionate. We end up generating a lot of heat, but very little light! The church has not been a stranger to that dynamic, from the time of the Acts of the Apostles until now.

We must face the reality of sin within the community. And here it is that we get into difficulty, for my perception of the sin involved may be different from yours. Not only will we differ about what constitutes the sin, but we may be unaware of the way in which our response to what we believe are the sins of others is itself sinful. After a passage in which the diversity within the church with its varieties of gifts is recognized, Paul goes on to "show a still more excellent way." First Corinthians 13 is often read at weddings; it is easy to talk about love in that setting. But the context in life for the passage is dissension within the church, and it is hard to act in love when either (1) what you believe to be crucial to Christian faith and life is threatened or (2) your faithfulness as a disciple of Jesus Christ is being called into question—especially when you do not deny what you are accused of being but do not believe it is sinful.

Yet I am convinced that if we cannot be the church in the midst of such situations, we are found wanting. In this, we will need the help of the Spirit for it is easy to become arrogant when we are passionate. We need to cultivate the capacity to really listen to those with whom we disagree, without surrendering the responsibility to clarify our position, and express our disagreement in ways that enable understanding rather than ways which inflame feelings. Every day I pray: God, "bring your healing grace to the whole church."[4]

Christian Experience

Although I have chosen to talk about Christian experience last, I must confess that its influence came very early in my journey in this area. My first encounter with homosexuals who shared the nature of their sexual identity with me could not have involved two more different people. One was a young man with serious emotional problems. Before I knew of his orientation, I had questions about his fitness for ministry. I did know he was not a whole person.

Another was a young woman with many gifts for ministry. She was a leader in campus religious life. She was our children's favorite baby-sitter. The grace of God was evident in her life. When she revealed that she was a lesbian, I discovered that my sense of her gifts for ministry did not change. God's Spirit bore witness with her spirit that she was a child of God, called to minister in Christ's name. After a brief period of reflection, my spouse and I did not hesitate to continue entrusting our children to her care. Because we knew her as a person, our trust in her concern for them and our knowledge of her love for Christ and the Church enabled us to begin to move in our understanding of homosexuality. And for that, I give thanks to God.

Again and again I have discovered rich resources for ministry from homosexuals whom I have known and with whom I have worked. Their love of God, their commitment to the Church in the presence of incredible ambiguity and pain, their caring and compassion for God's hurting children make it impossible for me to deny their calling. They have not been perfect people, any more than the heterosexuals with whom I have worked. But it has seemed clear to me that the healing and forgiveness they need is not based on their sexual orientation.

There are others—both homosexuals and heterosexuals—for whom the same thing could not be said. They have not seemed as healthy or gifted for ministry as the Church demands. Their sexuality (or their fear of it) is a cause of concern. Their need for healing and forgiveness is deep.

But among the others (and they are by far the larger group), I cannot deny the presence of the fruit of the Spirit in their ministry. I experience the presence of God at work in their lives as they minister in Christ's name. I stand with them because to stand against them would be to refuse to go where God has led me.

Why do I stand where I stand? Because I cannot with integrity do otherwise. *Veni Sancte Spiritus!* Come, Holy Spirit, and lead us all into your Truth beyond our knowing and our doing.

Notes

1. *The Book of Discipline of The United Methodist Church* (1996), paragraphs 65-76.

2. Ibid., paragraph 65G.

3. Ibid.

4. See any volume of *The Daily Office: A Book of Hours for Daily Prayer After the Use of the Order of Saint Luke* (Akron, Ohio: Order of Saint Luke Publications).

Homosexuality, Resistance, and the Social Principles

Chapter 4   *E. Dale Dunlap*

Homosexuality and the Social Principles

A brief word about the history of the issue of homosexuality in the now United Methodist Church may be useful in looking at its treatment in the Social Principles. Legislation regarding homosexuality had its beginning in the General Conference of 1972 in Atlanta. A Study Commission had been established at the Uniting Conference in 1968 to prepare a new statement on Social Principles. The statement on human sexuality was the most difficult of all to resolve. The Study Commission, responding to arguments from legal and medical professionals, recognized homosexuals as "persons of sacred worth who need the ministry and guidance of the Church" and whole "human and civil rights need to be ensured." But as Kenneth E. Rowe has observed, "the Conference voted with the people back home in affirming that the Church does not condone the practice of homosexuality and considers it 'incompatible with Christian teaching.' "[1] One of the most persuasive arguments offered on the floor seems to have been that "if we do not pass this legislation, we will lose members to the Southern Baptist Church." There is little evidence that biblical, theological, or ethical insights informed the discussion then. The present legislation was assembled by bits and pieces at various subsequent General Conferences with no apparent attempt at a holistic, consistent position, with still no serious systematic consideration being given to biblical, theological, or ethical insights. Finally, in 1988 General Conference established a "Committee to Study Homosexuality," and then proceeded to ignore its findings and recommendations. The recent ruling of the Judicial Council with regard to ceremonies that celebrate homosexual unions is an invitation to take a hard, critical look at what the Social Principles have to say about homosexuality.

At the outset I need to identify what I understand to be the official ground rules of The United Methodist Church that apply in such a dialogue as this.

First, it is a fundamental historical principle of Wesleyan and United Methodist dialogue that in matters of theological reflection we honor and practice "diversity in unity."[2] We hold a common core of "doctrine," but with no official interpretation of any doctrine. There is room for diversity of understanding. The issue of homosexuality certainly is not doctrine, and therefore this principle applies to our discussion of it.

Second, in *The Book of Discipline* there is articulated a principle of scriptural exegesis to be used by United Methodists. In light of the Judicial Council ruling and the rationale offered by the College of Bishops of the South Central Jurisdiction, which seems to have been accepted by the Council, consistence would require affording this exegetical principle the status of law, with any violation of it being a chargeable offense. The *Discipline* states:

> We are aided by scholarly inquiry and personal insight, under the guidance of the Holy Spirit. As we work with each text, we take into account what we have been able to learn about the original context and intention of that text. In this understanding we draw upon the careful historical, literary, and textual studies of recent years, which have enriched our understanding of the Bible. (par. 63, p. 76)

I would observe at this point that if this is taken seriously, none of the scriptural texts offered as proof that scripture condemns homosexuality are relevant to the issue. I would also observe that The United Methodist Church has consistently ignored and violated its own exegetical principles when it comes to the issue of homosexuality or same-gender orientation.

Third, the *Discipline* provides theological guidelines for use in discerning religious knowledge and authority (par. 63, pp. 74-80). It identifies the primacy of scripture (although not its exclusivity) "illuminated by tradition, vivified in personal experience, and confirmed by reason." In several places within the text it underlines the *interaction* of these four sources.

The Judicial Council Decision

The following is the text of the Judicial Council Decision with regard to the celebration of homosexual unions:

> The prohibitive statement in Par. 65C of the 1996 *Discipline*: "Ceremonies that celebrate homosexual unions shall not be conducted by our ministers and shall not be conducted in our churches," has the effect of church law, notwithstanding its placement in Par. 65C, and, therefore, governs the conduct of the ministerial office. Conduct in violation of this prohibition renders a pastor liable to a charge of disobedience to the order and discipline of The United Methodist Church under Par. 2624 of the *Discipline*.

This ruling is a fact, whether one likes it or not.

This ruling is curious at best. There is no question about General Conference passing the legislation. But the Council's "notwithstanding its placement in Par. 65C" is passing strange. Research of the *Minutes* of the 1996 General Conference makes it quite clear that General Conference deliberately chose to put the legislation in question in the Social Principles rather than in chapter 2 of the *Discipline* dealing with the ministry of ordained clergy or in the list of chargeable offenses found in chapter 7 on Judicial Administration. That option was offered as an amendment and was defeated by a vote of 553 to 321. How, then, can it be said that this legislation was not intended to be in the Social Principles under the rubrics in the preface of the Social Principles which condition the *whole* of the Social Principles:

> The Social Principles are a prayerful and thoughtful effort on the part of the General Conference to speak to the human issues in the contemporary world from a sound biblical and theological

foundation as historically demonstrated in United Methodist traditions. *They are intended to be instructive and persuasive in the best of the prophetic spirit.* The Social Principles are a call to all members of The United Methodist Church *to a prayerful, studied dialogue of faith and practice.*[3]

It strikes me that the Judicial Council has moved from interpreting the law (its responsibility) to action that is tantamount to making law (for which it does not have authority).

In the brief submitted by the College of Bishops of the South Central Jurisdiction, which argument apparently was persuasive for the Council, it was said that the placement of the prohibition in the Social Principles does not make it less a law. It was noted that other parts of the *Discipline* interact with the Social Principles. It was further held that "when the spirit and intent of the *Book of Discipline* is violated, all of the book is violated. . . . all of the book depends on each part of the book." All of this strikes me as questionable logic, as well as questionable exegesis of United Methodist history and polity. The implication seems to be that every statement of *The Book of Discipline* at least potentially constitutes a chargeable offense if disobeyed or disagreed with.

The Judicial Council has made its interpretation and decision. Surely it can be assumed that it applies consistently to all parts of the Social Principles. There is no defensible logic that permits picking and choosing which parts of the Social Principles are to be extrapolated and made into law.

A look at the consequences of a consistent application of this ruling to the whole of the Social Principles is instructive, if a little frightening. It would apply to anyone who:

1) does not oppose capital punishment and urge its elimination from all criminal codes (par. 68F)
2) opposes all forms and occasions of civil disobedience (par. 68E)
3) opposes the right of collective bargaining (par. 67B)
4) opposes basic human rights and civil liberties for homosexual persons (par. 66H)
5) opposes affirmative action as one method of addressing

the inequalities and discriminatory practices within our
Church and society (par. 66F)
6) opposes the United Nations and the International Court of
Justice (par. 69D)

There is much more.

An Inclusive Church

The United Methodist Church professes to be an inclusive
church. The Constitution states:

> The United Methodist Church is a part of the church universal,
> which is one Body in Christ. Therefore all persons, without regard
> to race, color, national origin, status, or economic condition, shall
> be eligible to attend its worship services, to participate in its pro-
> grams, and, when they take the appropriate vows, to be admitted
> into its membership in any local church in the connection. In The
> United Methodist Church no conference or other organizational
> unit of the Church shall be structured so as to exclude any member
> or any constituent body of the Church because of race, color,
> national origin, status, or economic condition. (Division One, par.
> 4, Article IV, p. 22)

The pertinent question for our concern at the moment is whether
one's gender orientation constitutes a status. In a 1993 ruling the
Judicial Council stated that there was no evidence that the word
"status" was intended to either include or exclude the clergy status of a self-avowed practicing homosexual. It went on to say that
"it is obvious that if the normal definition of 'status' is used, it
would be all inclusive." The same conclusion surely would apply
to laity as well. In point of fact, by the way in which we have dealt
with homosexuality we clearly have made it a "status."

The *Discipline*, par. 117, says:

> We recognize that God made all creation and saw that it was
> good. As a diverse people of God who bring special gifts and evi-
> dences of God's grace to the unity of the Church and to society, we
> are called to be faithful to the example of Jesus' ministry to all per-
> sons.

Inclusiveness means openness, acceptance, and support that enables *all* (emphasis added) persons to participate in the life of the Church, the community, and the world. Thus, inclusiveness denies every semblance of discrimination.

The mark of an inclusive society is one in which all persons are open, welcoming, fully accepting, and supporting of *all* (emphasis added) other persons, enabling them to participate *fully in the life of the* church (emphasis added), the community, and the world. . . .

In The United Methodist Church inclusiveness means the freedom for the *total involvement of all persons* (emphasis added) who meet the requirements of The United Methodist *Book of Discipline* in the membership and leadership of the Church at any level and in every place.

A further declaration of inclusiveness is found in *By Water and the Spirit*, "A United Methodist Understanding of Baptism" that was passed unanimously by the 1996 General Conference: "There are no conditions of human life (including age or intellectual ability, race or nationality, gender or sexual identity, class or disability) that exclude persons from the sacrament of baptism."[4] In this document baptism is entry into membership to the church—universal, denominational, and local. This is made clear also in Baptismal Covenants I and II, which were initially approved by General Conference in 1982, clearly identified as the official liturgical theology of The United Methodist Church by an overwhelming majority vote, and placed in *The United Methodist Hymnal* in 1989.

Do we need to be reminded that the constitutional and disciplinary professions of *all* in practice mean all *except* persons of same-gender orientation? So much for the gap between profession and actuality.

Par. 65C and Same-Gender Unions

The latest antihomosexual proscription to be added to the Social Principles says: "Ceremonies that celebrate homosexual unions shall not be conducted by our ministers and shall not be conducted in our churches" (par. 65C).

"We affirm that God's grace is available to all" (par. 65G) and we understand that God's grace is unconditional and prevenient, yet prohibiting the celebration of covenanted, faithful, loving unions of Christians of same-gender orientation does prohibit their participation *"fully* in the life of the church" (par. 117, emphasis added) and does deny them an important means of grace accorded to other Christians. "Refusing their request wrongly withholds a means of grace that opens pathways for God's Holy Spirit to transform not only them, but all of us into a Christian community more like the one Jesus envisioned in the Great Commandment."[5]

As we wrestle with the issue of same-gender unions we have to ask ourselves: is the essence of marriage in our Christian understanding a matter of gender and genital activity, or is it a covenant relationship of mutual fidelity and love? Instead of making a decision on the basis of abstract ideology, ought we not look at actual same-gender unions, particularly of professing and faithful Christians?—and there are such in reality whether the Church acknowledges them or not. Are they marked by covenanted, responsible, faithful, and lasting relationships? Do they show love for one another? Do they support one another "for richer or poorer; in sickness and in health"? In their relationship are they nurturing each other so as to move toward mutual self-fulfillment and the deepening of their relationship to God and other human beings? These are the characteristics we would say mark a true Christian union if they were heterosexual persons. Why, then, deny unions that display all of these characteristics and values just because the persons are same-gender oriented? I think Mr. Wesley would say at this point that the experience of reality, rather than abstract ideology, is the true test of a holy union. As the saying goes, if it looks like a duck, if it walks like a duck, if it quacks like a duck, it must be a duck.

Same-gender unions are no threat to nuclear families. The family in the Western world has been in trouble for a long time—and in deep trouble in the United States—but same-gender unions had nothing to do with this and must not be scapegoated for it. Actually, same-gender oriented unions represent an opposite trend. The desire of persons of same-gender orientation who wish for a committed, faithful union goes against the promiscuity of saunas and bathhouses and the Playboy culture that we decry. They are trying to form stable relationships and households. These Christians want to say, in the context of their Christian community, " 'Til death do us part."[6] We condemn the perceived promiscuity of many homosexuals but we apparently cannot bring ourselves to encourage, support, and rejoice in committed gay relationships that are fulfilling and redemptive. This, of course, is something that the majority of heterosexual culture cannot fathom. No one is denying that the faithful heterosexual marriage is a classical model or a paradigmatic case, but only saying that it does not exclude other models and cases.

The problem is one of discerning God's creative activity. If one begins, as I do, with a strong sense of God's continuing self-revelation, with a sense that God is still capable of surprises and that the Church's task is to respond in obedience to how God discloses God's self, the question becomes not an exegetical one—not what the scripture says, not what tradition says—but a hermeneutical one: What are the fruits of that relationship? Are they what are expected of a Christian union?

Ought not our basic interest to be in trying to discern what God is doing? It is a major mistake to regard creation as something that happened only in the distant past. Scripture and experience make clear that God is always doing new things. As Luke Timothy Johnson reminds us, "We need to keep in mind the way God has dealt in the past with God's precedents. The appearance of Jesus, the crucified Messiah, is a classic case of God operating outside God's own precedents. The inclusion of the Gentiles in the first generation of the church is another example. It was only after saying yes to God's activity among the Gentiles that the church began to figure out how this activity was in deep continuity with God's own plan."[7] Remember? The church taught that women were not equal to men, but God did a new thing. The church has condemned persons of same-gender orientation, and it is just possible that God is doing a new thing. In *The Book of Discipline* we say that the witness to our Lord and Savior Jesus Christ in the Church

> however, cannot fully describe or encompass the mystery of God.
> Though we experience the wonder of God's grace at work with

us and among us, and though we know the joy of the present
signs of God's kingdom, each new step makes us more aware of
the ultimate mystery of God, from which arises a heart of wonder and an attitude of humility. Yet we trust that we can know
more fully what is essential for our participation in God's saving
work in the world, and we are confident in the ultimate unfolding of God's justice and mercy. (par. 63, p. 83)

God is always doing new things.

There is something terribly wrong when two deeply spiritual,
mutually committed, faithful, and loving Christians cannot find
any place for their relationship within the Church. The Church
ought to at least entertain the replication of Peter's response to
the Holy Spirit being poured out on the household of Cornelius.
If God has accepted them, why shouldn't we? I must say that the
same-gender unions that I know about are as faithful and long
lasting as the heterosexual ones I observe.

On what gospel grounds, then, does the Church refuse to
bless such unions? We can bless buildings, choir robes, homes,
even pets—but we cannot bless a union of committed and faithful Christians who happen to be same-gender oriented. Do you
ever wonder what Jesus would think of this? Surely the Church
betrays its own redemptive ministry and reason for being when
it refuses to bless the union of two faithful Christian persons for
the sole reason that they are same-gender oriented.

A very strange flaw in our legislation is yet to be identified.
In withholding certain pastoral and liturgical ministries (means
of grace) from members who have been baptized with the same
baptism and have been received into membership in the Church
with the same profession and vows that apply to all United
Methodists, but who are persons of same-gender orientation,
the Church established a first-class membership and a second-
class membership—an action that is theologically, ecclesially,
and liturgically intolerable and indefensible.

Just as the legislation prohibiting the ordination of homosexual
persons negated the long-standing practice of the Church that left
the judgment about the qualifications of a person for ordination
as the responsibility of the annual conference, thus centralizing,
abstracting, and absolutizing the process, now this new legislation
circumscribes and restricts the pastoral office and ministry that

until now has been the responsibility of the pastor. What will be next? These are ominous steps moving The United Methodist Church toward a legalistic, dogmatic, authoritarian, and punitive orientation that is inconsistent with our Wesleyan heritage of unity in diversity of opinion—and this issue is not a doctrinal one and falls into the category Mr. Wesley spoke of as opinion.

Par. 65G and Human Sexuality

Before we can approach this paragraph with understanding, it is necessary to try to define homosexuality, or same-gender orientation. Homosexuality is not a concept that appears in the Bible and certainly cannot be identified as a "theme." The only thing the Bible speaks of, and then only seldom, is heterosexual men having "unnatural" relations with other, heterosexual men.

The word "homosexual" does not come into any language until the second half of the nineteenth century. There is no equivalent word in either Old Testament Hebrew or New Testament Greek. The concept of homosexuality was first given its name by the Hungarian, K. M. Benkert, in 1869, writing in the German language. Since the second half of the nineteenth century, we have become obsessed with homosexuality.

Homosexuality, or same-gender orientation, as generally understood today, is a sexual identity based upon a lifelong attraction, fixed early in life, toward persons of the same gender.

There is no simple answer to the question, What causes sexual orientation?—hetero or homo. Major theories cluster around two different approaches, the psychogenic and the genetic, with the arguments of neither being conclusive. Increasingly, however, research seems to be suggesting at least some element of genetic causation. What *is* clear, however, is that neither heterosexuality nor homosexuality is a deliberate, self-chosen orientation. Most persons have experienced their sexual orientation from early childhood. The great majority of homosexual persons do not appear to have meaningful choice concerning their orientation any more than do the great majority of heterosexual persons.

The 150,000 member American Psychological Association in August 1997 overwhelmingly passed a resolution reaffirming its long-standing position that homosexuality is not a mental disorder. They also opposed "all portrayal of Lesbian, Gay and Bisexual people as mentally ill and in need of treatment due to their sexual orientation." Nor is there any credible evidence that homosexuality is a medical illness. The association raises ethical concerns about any attempt on the part of psychologists to change their clients' orientations, and it specifically named "reparative therapy" as suspect. A year later, in 1998, the Board of the American Psychiatric Association unanimously rejected therapy aimed solely at turning gays into heterosexuals, saying it can cause depression, anxiety, and self-destructive behavior. It is its conclusion that the evidence would indicate this is the way people are born.

Nobody knows how to create sexual orientation. Therefore we cannot say that role modeling by parents or teachers, seduction, education, or any other experience determines or alters an individual's sexual orientation, either heterosexual or homosexual.

The mention of "reparative" or "conversion" therapy raises the fundamental issue of orientation versus behavior. A distinction is regularly made between a homosexual orientation and homosexual acts. It is conceded that orientation cannot be helped and may be accepted, but that homosexual acts or behavior are morally wrong. This is too neat a division between behavior and person.

Orientation is a given, not a choice, and is an essential ingredient of one's authentic being. Being is not an abstraction. It cannot be isolated from behavior. Being (orientation), to be real and visible, has to find expression in behavior. To separate the two is to create existential and moral schizophrenia. Such a distinction assumes that orientation is not all that important for what it means to be a person—which surely must be mistaken. To distinguish between orientation and behavior and to say that only behavior is morally decisive is to say, by implication, that orientation is morally irrelevant—which surely is unsupportable. All of this applies to heterosexuality and homosexuality alike.

If one recognizes and affirms the reality of same-gender orientation as "natural" to that person's being—as I think we have no other option if we follow our theological guidelines faithful-

ly—then to reject a "natural" expression of that orientation in
a covenantal, responsible, faithful, and loving relationship is
fundamentally immoral. It is tantamount to denying that person's right and responsibility to be her or his true self.

Separating orientation from behavior is a mistake, and so we
are forced to deal with this issue at a different level and in a different context.

Section G of paragraph 65 begins with the statement that "we
recognize sexuality is God's good gift to all persons." The desig-
nation of "all" is unambiguous and "sexuality" is not differenti-
ated. Homosexuality (same-gender orientation) is as much
"sexuality" as heterosexuality (other-gender orientation). Since
it is not a chosen orientation but seems to be in some real sense
a part of one's created nature, it would have to come under the
rubric of "God's gift" as being "good." I am not sure that we
really mean this. In light of the conclusion of the section that
condemns the practice of homosexuality it would appear that in
fact we mean that only "heterosexuality" is God's good gift.

This same section goes on to say that "we believe persons
may be fully human only when that gift [and this would mean
same-gender orientation, for those, who are, if we really do
mean that sexuality is God's good gift to all persons] is
acknowledged and affirmed by themselves, the church, and
society. We call all persons to the disciplined, responsible fulfillment of themselves, others, and society in the stewardship of
this gift. . . . All persons need the ministry and guidance of the
church in their struggles for human fulfillment, as well as the
spiritual and emotional care of a fellowship that enables reconciling relationships with God, with others, and with self."

Self-fulfillment, in this context, is an awesome and profound
concept. A gospel ethic can never forget that moral responsibility is intrinsically related to acceptance by significant others, and
ultimately by God. (In fact, acceptance by God is foundational.)
Life in Christ and human wholeness require self-acceptance and
self-acceptance requires a community of acceptance by others. It
is impossible for persons of same-gender orientation to have self-
acceptance or experience wholeness when their defining orientation is separated from behavior (a split personality). And what

they mostly experience is the kind of "acceptance" by others that accepts the orientation but not its natural, behavioral expression. Such "acceptance" is not an expression of Christian love. David M. Matzko suggests that we must:

> give a much deeper significance to orientation by focusing on the concept of complementarity. In other words, it is superficial to define homosexual orientation as an orientation toward a same-sex act or toward desire for a person of the same sex. . . . It has to do with how one comes to be a self in relation to others.
>
> Most accounts of marriage, for instance, suggest that the relationship between male and female enacts a completion of each person. I come to be who I am through the embodied presence of another.
>
> Though I may never engage in sexual intercourse, my orientation toward the other is constitutive of how I come to be a self in community. The term orientation identifies a basic category of the interaction between the self and world. At least that's what heterosexual orientation is usually considered to be.
>
> In these terms, homosexual orientation would not be merely a tendency toward a certain kind of act or a certain kind of desire. The true oddity of homosexuality—an oddity, that is for tradition—is that a person is oriented as a self through an other who is a person of the same sex. A person with a homosexual (same-gender) orientation comes to full fruition as a human being through an otherness and complementarity that is not of the opposite sex. The complementarity required for a person's "coming to be" is not founded on sexual differentiation, but it is still founded on a real "otherness."[8]

And for gay persons, accepting their orientation is accepting the way God has created them, and thus, in the deepest sense, the way of accepting God.

Section G makes clear that the Church has responsibility for providing a ministry that assists and enables persons of same-gender orientation in their struggle for human fulfillment, as well as providing the spiritual and emotional care of a fellowship that enables reconciling relationship with God, with others, and with self. I am afraid this does not describe The United Methodist Church that I know. The tragedy is that we seem to have no notion of the dynamics of human fulfillment for same-gender oriented persons, and we withhold the full support and ministry of a reconciling community.

Further along in this same section it is stated that "we insist that all persons, regardless of age, gender, marital status, or sexual orientation, are entitled to have their human and civil rights ensured." This is reiterated in detail in paragraph 66H. But we are unwilling to accord the full religious rights to members of The United Methodist Church who happen to be of same-gender orientation as we accord to other members. It is apparent that we expect higher standards of society than we are willing to accept for ourselves.

The final paragraph of Section G affirms that "homosexual persons no less than heterosexual persons are individuals of sacred worth." This affirmation is effectively negated by the subsequent prohibitive legislation. Homosexuality may be—is—of "sacred" worth (to God), but we do not value it that way, and I must tell you that in spite of our lofty declaration, persons of same-gender orientation, particularly our brothers and sisters in Christ, do not feel that the Church considers them to be "individuals of sacred worth," and they are in a position to better know than we are.

The climactic and defining statement of The United Methodist Church that conditions and defines the ultimate and *de facto* meaning and import of all other declarations, all of which are responsible and commendable taken at individual face value, negates them all with its unconditional and absolute judgment that it "does not condone the practice of homosexuality and considers this practice incompatible with Christian teaching." That is it; there is no more to be said. I would only enter the caveat that this statement is far from a consensus of the people called United Methodists, and that the matter is far from settled.

The postscript that "God's grace is available to all" has, for me, a very hollow ring to it, for God's grace is neither limited nor conditional, but by our own words and actions regarding same-gender oriented persons, we have conditioned and limited it by our own specifications.

A presumption underlying all of this legislation regarding persons of same-gender orientation is that homosexuality is a sin. Is it really? In Christian theology the basic and defining sin is separation and alienation from God. It is a fact that there are many same-gender oriented persons who are Christians, and by any credible gauge are not alienated from God any more than other-gender oriented (heterosexual Christians). Their lived faith and life in the Church bears witness to that fact. In the Wesleyan/United Methodist theological tradition, for something to be a sin requires the willful decision of the individual. Our best understanding of the nature of same-gender orientation is that it is not self-chosen and hence *cannot be identified as a sin.*

In light of all of this absolutistic and dogmatic stance, it is interesting to read in this same Section G that after all "we also recognize our limited understanding of this complex gift and encourage the medical, theological, and social science disciplines to combine in a determined effort to understand human sexuality more completely. We call the Church to take the leadership role in bringing together these disciplines to address this most complex issue."

. The General Conference did authorize in 1988 a Committee to Study Homosexuality, with the mandate to take account of the theological and ethical scholarship, seek the best biological, psychological, and sociological information and opinion. A representative and responsible committee did just this. At the close of their substantial report, the overwhelming majority of the committee concluded that certain assertions are true:

a) the seven biblical references and allusions cannot be taken as definitive for Christian teaching about homosexual practices because they represent cultural patterns of ancient society and not the will of God;

b) the scientific evidence is sufficient to support the contention that homosexuality is not pathological or otherwise an inversion, developmental failure, or deviant form of life as such, but is rather a human variant, one that can be healthy and whole;

c) the emerging scholarly views in biblical studies, ethics, and theology support a view that affirms homosexual relationships that are covenantal, committed, and monogamous;

d) the witness to God's grace of lesbian and gay Christians in the life of the Church supports these conclusions.[9]

They concluded their report with this recommendation:

The present state of knowledge and insight in the biblical, theological, ethical, biological, psychological, and sociological fields does not provide a satisfactory basis upon which the church can responsibly maintain the condemnation of all homosexual practice.[10]

As the General Conference has so often done, it chose to take no legislative action on the findings and recommendation of its own committee.

It is my perception that The United Methodist Church has come to a nonproductive dead end in our discussion of the issue of same-gender orientation. There is need for fresh, new ground for our discussion. I would propose, as a starter, four possible points of reference:

❑ First, that we devote our energies to trying to discern what God is doing in the Church and in the world without determining in advance what it is;

❑ Second, that we focus upon the meaning and reality of grace, with an openness to the guiding of the Holy Spirit that acts when, and where, and as it wills, and which, in our history as a people of God, does move in most unexpected ways that have a way of turning our own ways upside down;

❑ Third, that we explore the great biblical themes of oppression and freedom for insight and guidance; and

❑ Fourth, that we discuss sanctification. What does it mean to be a holy people? In a world where all fall short of the glory of God, what does it mean to be a good person? How does one become a better person?[11]

If we will make something like this our focus, it just may be that by the grace of God working through God's Holy Spirit we may yet be led into a "promising" land.

Notes

1. John G. McElhenney, ed. *United Methodism in America* (Nashville: Abingdon Press, 1992), p. 127.

2. *The Book of Discipline*, Par. 63, p. 81.

3. See Par. 509, Part III, Social Principles, Preface, p. 84 of *The Discipline* (emphasis added).

4. From *The Book of Resolutions of The United Methodist Church* (Nashville: The United Methodist Publishing House, 1996), pp. 716-35. Quote is on p. 726.

5. Jeanne Knepper and Morris Floyd in *Affirmation*, Fall, 1998, pp. 1-2.

6. Luke Timothy Johnson in "Homosexuality, Marriage and the Church: A Conversation," *Christian Century*, July 1-8, 1998, p. 649.

7. Ibid., p. 644.

8. David McCarthy Matzko in "Homosexuality, Marriage and the Church: A Conversation," p. 647.

9. *The Church Studies Homosexuality*, Study Book, Gary L. Ball-Kilbourne, ed. (Nashville: Cokesbury, 1994), p. 35.

10. Ibid., p. 36.

11. Acknowledgment is given to Alice Knotts, *Affirmation*, Fall 1998, p. 2, for contribution to the shaping of this paragraph.

Chapter 5

L. Edward Phillips

Homosexual Unions and the Social Principles

Blessing the Incompatible?

Item One:	"Although we do not condone the practice of homosexuality and consider this practice incompatible with Christian teaching, we affirm that God's grace is available to all" (1996 *Book of Discipline,* par. 65G).
Item Two:	"We believe war is incompatible with the teachings and example of Christ" (1996 *Book of Discipline,* par. 69C).
Item Three:	"Ceremonies that celebrate homosexual unions shall not be conducted by our ministers and shall not be conducted in our churches" (1996 *Book of Discipline,* par. 65C).
Item Four:	Blessing, For Those in Military Service: "Guard brave men and women in military service. . . . Though for a season they must be people of war, let them live for peace, as eager for agreement as for victory . . . and never let hard duty separate them from loyalty to your Son . . ." (*The United Methodist Book of Worship,* p. 542).[1]

The United Methodist Church is struggling with strong differences of opinion over homosexuality, with sincere and dedicated Christians on all sides of the issue. Some United Methodists are advocating schism as the unavoidable way to end the tension. Before we accept schism as inevitable, however, I suggest we consider, by way of comparison, another very important issue where the Church is similarly divided over its understanding of Christian teaching and the practice of United Methodists: the Church's position on war and service in the military.

It is only fair to acknowledge my commitments at the outset. I am a pacifist. I embrace pacifism, not because I think it is a good idea or even that it will make war less likely, but because as a disciple of Jesus I have been commanded to love my enemies and to do good toward them. I see it as a fundamental issue of Christian discipleship and commitment to the sovereignty of God.

The Social Principles in *The Book of Discipline* support me in my position. In addition to the quotation given in Item One above, the *Discipline* further states: "Though coercion, violence, and war are presently the ultimate sanctions in international relations, we reject them as incompatible with the gospel and spirit of Christ" (par. 68G). In this same paragraph, the *Discipline* offers support to those who "conscientiously oppose all war, or any particular war, and who therefore refuse to serve in the armed forces or to cooperate with systems of military conscription." It would seem that I have the Church's full support for my position: war and violence are incompatible with the teachings of Christ, and opposition to war and military service receives the Church's unconditional support.

Paradoxically, however, the very last sentence of paragraph 68G, in the *Discipline*, states: "We also support and extend the Church's ministry to those persons who *conscientiously choose* to serve in the armed forces or to accept alternative service" (emphasis added). In all honesty, I cannot see how it is possible for a Christian *conscientiously* to choose to go against the teachings of Christ. That is to say, I do not see how a person could reject violence and war as incompatible with the teachings of Christ, and then *conscientiously* choose to engage in war and violence. Yet, thousands of United Methodists do in fact join the

military and support their governments in armed conflict.
Clearly there are many United Methodists who sincerely believe
that they may enter the military as faithful Christians without
compromising their commitments to Christ or the Church. No
matter how hard I try, I cannot see how they come to this conclusion, even though I know from personal experience that
some of these United Methodists are sincere Christians who are
attempting to live faithful lives.

In support of Christians in the military, *The United
Methodist Book of Worship* contains a blessing "For Those in
Military Service."[2] This blessing acknowledges that "for a season" those Christians in the military will be "people of war." I
am troubled by the inclusion of this blessing in our *Book of
Worship*, since it asks God to bless a practice that our Social
Principles acknowledge is "incompatible with the teachings and
example of Christ." (I note with irony that there is no comparable blessing in our *Book of Worship* for women and men who
choose to oppose military service.) Even though I am an
ordained United Methodist minister, I could not in good conscience offer this blessing for someone in the military, even
though it is in our *Book of Worship*. Nevertheless, I would not
categorically bar fellowship with a United Methodist who is in
the military, nor would I bar fellowship with another pastor
who did use this blessing.

To summarize the points:

1) The Social Principles acknowledge that war is incompatible with the teachings of Christ.
2) Paradoxically, the Social Principles allow that some
Christians may decide that they could go to war.
3) The *Book of Worship* contains a blessing for persons who
make such a decision.

The similarities and differences between the ways the
Discipline addresses war and homosexuality are striking. The
Social Principles state that the practice of homosexuality, like the
practice of war, is incompatible with "Christian teaching." We
should notice here the phrase "Christian teaching," rather than

"teachings and example of Christ," as in the reference to war. This is due to the fact that we have no record that Jesus himself ever commented on the matter of homosexuality. Yet, despite the negative evaluation of the "practice of homosexuality," the Social Principles also acknowledge that homosexuals are persons of "sacred worth" who need the fellowship of the church (par. 65G). In the spirit of this second statement, I, along with many other United Methodists, affirm that many gay and lesbian couples conscientiously live out their sexuality with integrity as Christians, that is to say, as part of their faithful commitment to Christ. This is why some of us have asked that homosexual unions be blessed within the Church and to receive the support of the Christian community. Yet, the Social Principles state: "Ceremonies that celebrate homosexual unions shall not be conducted by our ministers and shall not be conducted in our churches" (par. 65C). Given the position of the Church on war and the blessing of men and women in the military, this seems to me to be ironic, if not hypocritical. Why should the Church be willing to bless the one supposed "incompatibility" and not the other?

Of course, I do not want to fall into the trap of trying to justify my position based on the precedent of a bad decision. If it is wrong for the Church to offer its blessing to military service which is incompatible with the teaching of Christ (as I believe it is), then someone who accepts the Social Principles' statements on homosexuality will undoubtedly offer the same argument right back as a reason why the Church ought not to conduct services of "holy union."

With regard to war, however, the fact is many United Methodists *do not* believe that war is fundamentally incompatible with the teachings of Jesus if it is a just war. Many United Methodists probably believe that it is the duty of Christians to go to war, and even to be willing to kill others, if the cause is just. Moreover, I suspect that some United Methodists would be willing to give their political and military leaders the benefit of the doubt regarding what constitutes a just war.

In like manner, those of us who support the blessing of homosexual unions do not believe that homosexuality is fundamentally incompatible with Christian teaching so long as it is held to the same standards of fidelity that (ostensibly) apply to hetero-sexual relationships. For the sake of argument, one could com-pare the reasoning that would lead one to accept participation in a just war with the reasoning that would lead one to accept homosexual unions. Briefly, let me suggest how this reasoning might work. The New Testament norm for heterosexual rela-tionships would be the faithful sexual union of husband and wife, and the New Testament standard for the treatment of ene-mies would be to love and do good to them, forsaking the sword of retribution. Sexual sinning would include fornication (sex between unmarried persons) or adultery, and also sexual inter-course that is forced, even between husband and wife, or with-held within marriage without due reason. Similarly, war as it is generally practiced (that is, wars which do not meet the criteria of "just" war, wars of aggression, or wars which cannot protect noncombatants, etc.) would also be forbidden to Christians, and even in the most justifiable circumstances would still be the less-er of evils. A homosexual union, finally, would be comparable (in this line of reasoning) to the just war position. It would be justifiable given the circumstances, if it can meet certain criteria. For a just war, the criteria would include discrimination in the use of violence to protect the innocent, justness of the cause, the probability of success, and so forth. In the case of homosexual unions, the criteria would include the standards of fidelity, mutu-ality, and monogamy that apply to marriage.

Now, I am sure that those who support homosexual unions (as I do) will be quite uncomfortable with my comparison with just war thinking. Obviously, engaging in a sexual relationship is by no means comparable to killing another human being. But, the foremost objection would be that gays and lesbians seek the support of the Church for their committed unions, not as a con-solation prize, but as a celebration of their love and commit-ment. It simply will not work to say, "We really are sinning here, but given the circumstances, we believe that God will allow us this as a lesser of evils." Rather, gay and lesbian Christians and others of us who support them want the Church to recognize their commitments as *holy* unions that are *intrinsi-cally open to God's blessing and the support of the Church.*

Yet, I suspect that many of those who support Christians in the military and who want their military service blessed would have a similar concern for their position—they seek the blessing of the Church as a celebration of their commitment to a "holy" honor, duty, and personal sacrifice, not merely as the lesser of evils. We really can never be satisfied with "blessing" what we actually believe is "incompatible" with the gospel.

This is one of the reasons why I think that the position of those who support military service for Christians is untenable. Nevertheless, I am willing to remain in The United Methodist Church with those who support the military, because, all things considered, I would much rather my Christian brothers and sisters attempt to take a conscientious approach to their military service than to give themselves to such service uncritically. As a Christian pacifist, I believe it is my responsibility to keep reminding them that the criteria of just war are stringent and must be taken seriously. Likewise, I would hope that those who oppose homosexual practice would see that, all things considered, at the very least it is much better for our gay and lesbian brothers and sisters to be in faithful, monogamous homosexual unions with the support of their Church, than to struggle against the dangerous and idolatrous cultural tide of sexual promiscuity without such support. That is to say, it might be helpful for those who oppose homosexual unions to embrace a line of thinking similar to the just war position as a way to acknowledge such unions within the Church, even though they are not satisfied that these unions should be blessed by the Church. I must also expect that they would keep raising questions about Christian commitment to fidelity and monogamy, not only for our gay and lesbian brothers and sisters, but for all of us.

But here is the central, and most difficult, point in my argument: those who support holy unions should be concerned with the same questions about fidelity and monogamy. For, while we can only bless what we believe is compatible with the gospel of Jesus Christ, we must never forget that the gospel is not primarily about affirmation, but *conversion*. We ask God to bless our commitments to each other so we may be transformed[3] into a sign of God's utterly faithful, noncoercive, gratuitous, holy and creative Kingdom, which exposes the idolatry and domination inherent in all human systems and institutions—including marriage. Therefore, the Church has no business giving its approval to holy unions in order for them to be a duplication of marriage, per se. Rather, the Church should ask God to bless holy unions in order for them to be an image of Christ's holy union with the church. As such, the blessing of holy unions becomes a prophetic act of the gospel of Jesus Christ before the world. I suggest that one reason there is such resistance to the blessing of holy unions among some Christians is that such unions expose how marriage among heterosexual Christians too often fails to embody just this prophetic witness to the gospel.

Let me summarize my argument.

1) As Christians we can only bless what we believe to be compatible with the gospel.
2) The United Methodist Church as a whole displays confusion in regard to both homosexuality and war (and also on other matters which we have not discussed here).
3) We seek God's blessing in order to transform our human actions into sign of the kingdom of God.
4) We do not have to embrace fully the position of those with whom we disagree on these points in order to live together in fellowship as we seek to resolve the Church's confusion.

I must confess that as I have shared these ideas with my gay and lesbian friends some of them have been less than impressed. Why should they remain in a church with persons (some of whom will be the preachers and teachers) that do not fully embrace them as God made them? I will refrain from offering the advice, "Be patient," because I am painfully aware such advice has been offered to legitimate ongoing sexism and racism. How can we "be patient" when we believe the Church is being unfaithful to the gospel? And, yet, I am also aware of how "impatient" women and persons of color, working within the Church, have gradually begun to change the way the

Church understands itself as an inclusive community. Theologically, I believe this is how the Holy Spirit works within us and among us through "loyal opposition" to form us all into the Body of Christ.

Here is my modest proposal for a way beyond our impasse. Let us commit to live together in a church in which we call each other to account for all the ways we struggle to live out our dedication to the gospel in our harsh and complex world, so that we may come to see where we have strayed in our dedication to Jesus Christ. As a sign of this commitment, just as the Church has made room in its *Book of Worship* for the blessing of soldiers, let us similarly make room for those who, out of their understanding of the gospel, conscientiously choose to honor holy unions. For if we can hold our differences about war in tension, how much easier should it be to hold homosexuality in tension within the Church as we seek God's will. In the meantime, I will allow you to give your blessings when you are convinced in your heart that you are doing the right thing, if you will allow me to do the same.

Notes

1. *The United Methodist Book of Worship* (Nashville: The United Methodist Publishing House, 1992).
2. The source for this blessing is the *Presbyterian Worshipbook*.
3. I realize this word has been co-opted by the so-called "Transforming Congregations" movement to signify the supposed "healing" of persons of homosexual orientation. I can only say that our Christian vocabulary is always open to misuse.

RESISTANCE AND HUMAN RIGHTS

Chapter 6

Gilbert Haven Caldwell

The Last Prejudice

On October 12, 1998, I participated in a vigil for Matthew Shepard on the steps of the Colorado State Capitol in Denver. Matthew Shepard was the young gay man who was brutally assaulted and left to die, tied to a fence in Laramie, Wyoming. I was the first speaker at that gathering, and I shared these words:

> As a United Methodist clergyman who is African American, I had hoped that in 1998 we had ceased lynching persons because of the way they looked, or what their sexual orientation might be, or for any other reason. The beating and death of Matthew Shepard indicates my hopes were premature. May persons of all faith traditions, and those who profess no religious faith, declare an end to the practice of stereotyping any person or group. May all of us work harder to end the hate and stop the violence.

I recall that moment in history with its painful memories that are still with many of us, because in my comments I felt it necessary to articulate my African Americanness, despite the fact that from visual observation my race was obvious. I am concerned that so many of my colleagues in the struggle for racial justice, persons with whom I marched, persons who found themselves in Mississippi with me during that exhilarating and dangerous "Freedom Summer," and most of those with whom I

99

experienced arrests and brief detention, have been so *ominously* silent in response to the struggles of gay, lesbian, bisexual, and transgender persons.

Often I have heard them quote Scripture in ways comparable to the ways Scripture was and is used to declare and define the second-class human status of those of us of African descent. William H. Willimon writes: "Much of the Bible is story and a great deal of it is poetry. Be careful with poetry. It is more than just sweet, religious thoughts. It has a subversive political function. By singing the Bible's songs, an old, established order is being dismantled and a new order is being put in its place."[1]

If any people know how the Bible has been used to serve a "political function," it ought to be those of us who have been and still are on a journey from slavery to freedom. We have known biblical usage that has enslaved us, but we have also known biblical usage that has been a centerpiece of our liberation struggle.

Vincent Harding, writing about David Walker and *Freedom's Journal,* the first black newspaper in America, asks, "What is the role of the word—the spoken word, the preached word, the whispered-in-the-night-time word, the written word, the published word—in the fight for black freedom?"[2] My colleagues and I, who contribute to this work, seek to offer candid, controversial commentary on resistance to the historic resistance— of religious life in general, and United Methodism in particular—to sisters and brothers whose sexual orientation is other than heterosexual. I offer my words, with the hope that the reader will become a coparticipant and cocreator with me in an improvisational mode—like music of the jazz musician—and improvise more profound thoughts from the reader.

The church, born with the label of heretic in the first century, has become amazingly fearful of contemporary "resistance movements" that challenge the status quo. Hans Küng in his classic, *The Church,* reminds us of the early history of the community of faith: "The very fact that the young Church was itself regarded as 'heretical' must have made it cautious and wary in its relations with heretics." Why, where, and how have we lost our caution about declaring movements and perspectives that diverge from "mainstream" thinking, heretical? We are so sure in our pronouncements about the "incompatibility" of homosexuality, even as we know that in so many ways the Church has been led, shaped, and molded for the better by persons whose sexual orientation is so labeled. There is a crying need for us to eradicate our capacity for denial and eliminate the hypocrisy that limits and restricts our capacity for healthiness.

How sad it is that a denomination that allowed itself to be divided over the right or wrong of human slavery, continues to oppress, disenfranchise, bring to trial and dismiss those who are on the "wrong side" as they claim their sexuality, or as they advocate the right of persons to express their nonheterosexual sexuality. Some of us have decided to say to our beloved United Methodism, "Before I'll be a slave, I'll be buried in my grave, and go home to my Lord and be free."

We must resist because we have not understood how our reluctance to affirm sexuality—heterosexual and homosexual—creates a spiritual wasteland, a spiritual emptiness, a spiritual incompleteness that restricts and constricts our spiritual capacity and possibility. Thomas Merton suggests, "The whole purpose of spiritual direction is to penetrate beneath the surface of a [person's] life, to get behind the facade of conventional gestures and attitudes which [he or she] presents to the world and to bring out . . . inner spiritual freedom . . . inmost truth, which is what we call the likeness of Christ in [one's] soul."[3] We have allowed our debates, our decisions, and our hiding behind litigation (charges, trials, suspensions, and dismissals) to rob us of "the inner spiritual freedom" that Merton describes.

Billy Taylor, the gifted jazz pianist, composer, educator, and CBS contributor, wrote a song many years ago that spoke of freedom. Some in the Church and society are saying, "I wish I knew how it feels to be free, to break all the chains that are holding me." We have not dared calculate the spiritual costs that have been ours because of our limiting of the God-given humanity of women, of persons of African descent, and of those whose sexual orientation does not meet the facade "of conventional gestures and attitudes." Years ago, as I was leading a workshop on racism, a young white pastor explained why he felt called and compelled to assist his congregation in eradicating racism. He said that at the major hospital located in their urban setting, his white congregants would more than likely encounter persons of color. He said, "It is awful enough for my members to experience cancer in their bodies, they ought not also carry with them the cancer of racism."

Through the ages the church in its efforts to regulate human behavior, particularly sexual behavior, has done great damage to God's creative activity as expressed in human creation. Our fears have shaped our projections. It is said that those who have been abused have a greater propensity for becoming abusers. Our personal sexual uncertainty has been expressed by our declarations of certainty about the sinfulness of homosexual orientation. We have a "compatibility" problem when it comes to the Creator's gift of sexuality. Our problem is made manifest in our declaration of the practice of homosexuals as "incompatible with Christian teaching." A denomination, able to achieve with God's help what we have achieved and accomplished can, must, and will find a way to resolve our differences. But this resolution will occur only as we United Methodists practice our own version of "Truth and Reconciliation," an expression of truth that results in reconciliation.[4]

An insightful essay on homosexuality by Peter I. Gomes, Preacher to Harvard University, fires my growing commitment to encourage, cajole, prod, and challenge my denomination, the Christian establishment, and society in general. On homosexuality, which Gomes calls "the last prejudice," he states:

> Unlike the topics of other moral debates, homosexuality is seen not only as a social practice or condition upon which good hearts and minds may differ but as an issue so central to right conduct and belief that compromise or sweet reasonableness is thought to be capitulation to error, and therefore unacceptable. Thus, the debate is almost undebatable. . . . What is at stake is not simply the authority of scripture, as conservative opponents to homosexual legitimization like to say, but the authority of the culture of interpretation by which these people read in such a way as to lend legitimacy to their doctrinaire prejudices.[5]

Homosexuality and same-sex unions, more than race, gender or divorce, challenge what Gomes calls "the authority of scripture" and "the authority of the culture of interpretation." Human beings want to change without changing. This is why we find it difficult, even within the Christian community, to confess, repent, restore, and recommit on the issue of homosexuality. To do so is to acknowledge that "we [saw] through a glass dimly" at one time during our journey. We want to "sneak up" on change, so that no one will notice. This approach, however, permits and prompts reversal and regression of recent "correctives"—for example, affirmative action—thus we establish a cycle of discussion, debate, change, and then resistance and retreat, over and over again.

Resolution and reconciliation within the Church on homosexuality offer us the opportunity to "become honest" before the world, acknowledging that our response to living Scriptures and to a God who is involved and engaged in continuing and unfolding revelatory activity, has made the Church and will make the Church, a dynamic and changing community/institution.

I offer this illustration in the form of an individual and a particular moment in history. Along with an uncle and my father, I was named after Gilbert Haven (1821–1880), a white Methodist clergyman who became a bishop. In his role as editor of the *Zion's Herald,* the conference newspaper, Haven was unceasing and untiring in his commitment to racial equality and interracial marriage. The time in which he lived was as divided on matters of race, as our time is divided on homosexuality. He not only prophetically proclaimed the rightness and righteousness of racial equality and justice, he had the audacity to be publicly proactive on the correctness of interracial marriage.[6] Our beloved Methodism, with all of its many denominational manifestations, is longing for leadership from pulpit to pew; from probationers to bishops that will dare run the risk of dissenting from the stifling status quo of exclusivity and proclaim the word and lead the movement toward affirmation and inclusivity of our sisters and brothers, known and unknown, whose sexual orientation is labeled homosexual. Where are those who have led and are still in the forefront on other justice issues? Where are those of all races who regret that they were too young or too preoccupied or too "not-yet-convinced" to witness in Mississippi, or march from Selma to Montgomery or in Washington. Where are those who feel called to "stand up" for persons who are unlike themselves but whose humanity is as precious as theirs? Where are those who believe that the Church, in order to witness with integrity, must witness to a Creator who is "not finished with any of us yet"? Where are those whose passions draw them to the economic and power imbalances in our nation and our world, who believe that our fascination with sexual orientation, sexuality, and sexual issues divert us from the deeper and wider divisions within the human family? Where are your words and actions that let us know we have wasted so much time on this issue, while millions are dying because of the violence of poverty, hunger, disease, and group conflict? Where are those persons who correctly remind us of our capacity to misunderstand proportionality, thus causing us to "major in minors, and minor in majors"?

In her Protestant Hour sermon "We Are One in the Spirit, Aren't We?"[7] Carol Matteson Cox tells the story of that World War II time when the Nazis were about to invade Denmark. The plan was to kill the Jews who would be identified by the Star of David they would be ordered to wear. To thwart this plan the King of Denmark ordered all Danish citizens to wear the yellow star. "Because the Danes stood together (Jew and non-Jew), the Nazi plan was stymied" (p. 54). We know that during that awful moment in history, as Jews were being "exterminated," so were homosexuals. We still cringe in disbelief as we reluctantly understand the complicity of Christians and the church in the Holocaust. But our silence in the presence of those who declare homosexual behavior incorrect and inappropriate makes us accomplices to a more subtle extermination today.

Some of us have decided to resist prevailing negative sentiments and attitudes in church and community on homosexuality, to stand with our gay, lesbian, bisexual, and transgender colleagues. We believe that racial justice is achieved only as white persons "stand" with people of color. So it is with the justice struggles of those whose orientation is labeled homosexual. Liberation, freedom, justice, and movement from invisibility to visibility occur in proportion to the number of persons willing to stand for, with, and on behalf of sisters and brothers who are demeaned, dismissed, and denied because of their sexual orientation. The most effective attitude, the most faithful resistance, is for us to understand that "we are family." We are members and citizens of the same human village. It takes the awareness and practice of being a human family living in a world village, called into being by the Creator God to transform us for effective resistance and faithful living in a new century.

Notes

1. *Shaped by the Bible* (Nashville: Abingdon Press, 1990), p. 73.

2. *There Is a River: The Black Struggle for Freedom in America* (New York: Vintage, 1982), p. 82. (New York: Image, 1976), p. 314.

3. *Spiritual Direction and Meditation and What Is Contemplation?* (Anthony Clarke, 1975), p. 17.

4. This is the name of a commission headed by Bishop Desmond Tutu in South Africa. With all the obvious limitations of that commission it nevertheless poses in the language of its name a model for the United Methodists to emulate.

5. "The Bible and Homosexuality: The Last Prejudice," chapter 8, in *The Good Book, Reading the Bible Mind and Heart* (New York: William Morrow, 1996), pp. 145 and 162.

6. See William B. Gravely, *Gilbert Haven, Methodist Abolitionist* (Nashville: Abingdon Press, 1973).

7. *Jubilee Time, Celebrating God's Grace and Justice* (Nashville: Abingdon Press, 1984).

LIFE IN THE CHURCH AS RESISTANCE

Chapter 7 *Jeanne Audrey Powers*

"*The Journey*"
A Sermon
Scripture: Exodus 1:8–2:15

Introduction to the Sermon

The sermon that follows was preached at the 1995 Convocation of the Reconciling Congregations Program, held in Minneapolis in July of that year. The Convocation theme was "Bound for the Promised Land."

My "coming out" in this sermon created considerable publicity in both the secular and church media, no doubt because I had developed a careful strategy to be as public as possible in this action. I do not recommend this action for everyone, but several factors played a role in my doing this.

At the time I was in my twenty-second year as a staff person in one of our national United Methodist agencies and in my thirty-seventh year as an ordained member of the Minnesota Annual Conference. I had frequently been related to controversial issues. I had developed expertise in my position and in many issues of concern to the general church, that is, I was not a "one-issue" person. I was widely known and respected throughout the denomination.

As I said in an accompanying statement, "This action today is 'a political act.' It is an act of resistance to false teachings that have contributed to heresy and homophobia within the Church

109

itself. It is a statement not of withdrawal or disillusionment, but rather an affirmation that the Church is also a gift of God. (In an earlier part of the statement I had named my sexuality as 'a good gift from God.') Believing that, I will never give up on it, even in its institutional form."

An important element of this act was to disseminate it as widely as possible. I therefore developed, in advance, a packet consisting of the sermon, a personal statement explaining why I was doing this, a detailed biographical page indicating various roles I had played in the Church, and a press release. This was sent, in advance, to about thirty secular newspapers and magazines and about twenty-five religious magazines and journals throughout the country. My action was widely covered in both of the Minneapolis and St. Paul newspapers, on three Twin Cities television stations that day, and later in newspaper articles and editorials around the country. Most of these media quoted from my personal statement and interviews with me; religious magazines included direct quotes from my sermon, as well.

I believe my intentions were accomplished. I wanted to show that gay and lesbian clergy (and laypeople, of course) could—and do—have a record of faithful discipleship and Christian commitment, and that that self-understanding was not a detriment to their witness or to their service in the church. Before the time of public knowledge of "services of holy union," it was one more way of initiating serious conversation about the official positions of the denomination and the place of gays and lesbians in the life of the Church.

In a more personal way, I saw it as developing "cognitive dissonance" among persons who held a conservative perspective on homosexuality, especially in the church. Those who had come to know and respect my leadership were required to acknowledge this "new information" and to decide for themselves whether my sexual orientation therefore contradicted the high regard they had previously had for me. In "giving a personal face" to people previously seen in a "category," I hoped that more open, realistic, and progressive understandings might result.

The Sermon

On Good Friday of this year, I participated in an extraordinary journey. Beginning with a rosary service in Santa Cruz, New Mexico, I made "the Walk" to Santuario de Chimayo, along with some 30,000 others in Northern New Mexico. A pilgrimage: whole families; groups of young people; parents pushing baby carts; an adult son helping his father who had just come through a severe heart attack; a blind man with his seeing-eye dog. Some carried large crosses over their backs, others small crucifixes in their hands. It was a Mexican Catholic expression of spirituality with its American adaptation. In some cases, as we headed for Chimayo, we were "bound for the Promised Land," to that little church, sacred space for thousands of the faithful.

People walked as far as they knew they were able; some from over one hundred miles away; others, just all night long. But each of us walked, carrying inside of us "our intentions" as part of the journey. Some walked with intentions for their sick relatives, some for peace in the world, some for blessings in undertaking a new job, others for perseverance and determination to hold steady in the face of every obstacle.

I walked with the "intentions" of this convocation, remembering that even though Scripture tells us that while we may not live in the Promised Land, we shall see it! So I want to speak today about the Walk, the Journey, the Way. We may think we are still in Egypt, a Hebrew word that also means "a place of constriction" (in contrast to the wide open spaces of the wilderness and the abundance of the promised land). No wonder we call it liberation! But we have begun the walk, a "long night's journey into day."[1] And it is about that journey that I want to speak.

Women, only recently, have been uncovering stories that have been hidden from them in Scripture, and I found one as I was reflecting on this sermon. It's a woman's story, but with special relevance, I believe, for all of us attending this convocation. Pay close attention to the text! The Hebrew midwives engage in a lie, deliberately telling Pharaoh what was not true about the pregnant

Hebrew women; the mother of Moses is deceptive and hides
Moses in a floating basket; the daughter of the Pharaoh defies her
father's orders that all Hebrew boy babies be killed; Moses' own
sister operates under pretense and gets Pharaoh's daughter to
allow the baby to go "back to his mother's arms and breast."
Later, Pharaoh's daughter falsely claims she is his mother. Do you
notice the action words that describe these women? The midwives lie, Moses' mother is deceptive, Pharaoh's daughter defies
orders and later makes false claims, and Moses' sister operates
under pretense. These are all extremely brave women in the face
of Pharaoh's power. Their perseverance and determination saves
the life of Moses, who enables the Hebrew people to be freed
from their bondage. A powerless people are transformed into a
self-determining nation. Indeed, these heroic women model for us
liberation from constriction, using subversion to transform the
faith community.

There is yet a little more to be said. In the passage that follows,
when Moses, as an adult, happens upon an Egyptian beating a
Hebrew, he kills the Egyptian. But notice what he does first. The
text says, "He looked this way and that, and seeing no one
[Moses] killed the Egyptian" (Exod. 2:11-12). Smart man: His
question was, "Am I going to get caught?" The next day he con-
fronts two Hebrews fighting amongst themselves, only to be told,
"Butt out. Who allowed you, a murderer, to judge us?" Realizing
that word has gotten out about the killing, Moses escapes to
Midian, lest Pharaoh realize that there has been a Hebrew in his
own palace all the time.

A subversive strategy is emerging—deception; operating
under pretense; and making false claims. And let's add three
more descriptions of this resistance strategy: (1) don't get
caught; (2) when you know it is the right time, don't hesitate to
confront; (3) and flee when you have to!

Now I know the Church has never used these words in any
kind of positive way at all. In fact, if anything, these words tend
to be found more in our confessional prayers than in our calls
to action. But since the Reconciling Congregations Program is a
resistance movement, and that's exactly what the women in this
story were, let's see if we can unpack the words we don't like

and think again about the miraculous way Yahweh worked through these women.

When I was in the missionary personnel office of the Board of Global Ministries in the very early 70s, one young man with a developing career in banking made application. He was seeking to become a US-2 as a conscientious objector to the Vietnam War. I asked him why he was coming to the Church for employment, and he replied, "Because it's the only institution I know that pays its employees to be subversive." I have never forgotten that high tribute to the Church. Because we seek to overcome powers and principalities of this world, even when they are in the Church, our vocational call is to be subversive.

For four months of this year, I was on study leave, and my focus was on the Holocaust, or the *Shoah*, as it is usually called in Jewish circles. I was particularly interested in the kind of people who were involved in it. A book title describes them as *Perpetrators, Victims, and Bystanders*. Some authors categorize them as "Unrighteous and Righteous Christians, Survivors, and Rescuers."

Over and over again I was moved by the diaries and first-person accounts of survivors and rescuers. Confronted with the demonic evil minds of the perpetrators (who usually loved their wives and children, took pride in their gardens, and played Mozart at the end of a day's work), these survivors and rescuers only lived one day at a time. They knew that in order to live to see the promised land, they would need to be subversive, to deliberately resist unjust authority, sometimes perpetrated by their own people.

As I read about resisters and survivors during the time of Holocaust horrors, I kept thinking about what it means to be truly subversive to the Church's unjust life and teaching about homosexuality. As long as the phrases "homosexuality and the Christian faith are incompatible," and "celibacy in singleness" continue to stand in our *Discipline,* no matter how these phrases are introduced or framed, our Church is on record as perpetuating heterosexism in its life and homophobia in its teaching.

So I began to see some parallels between the behavior of some persons during the Nazi era and the way some straight and gay and lesbian people act in the Church today. Each of these four ways of being are based on the choices we make, and each of us, straight or gay, is required to make them daily.

1. One choice is to be a "bystander." Frightened by possible consequences in the Nazi era, they kept silent. Today, you can be sure they would never dare to show up at this convocation, or visit the Names quilt, or even make an anonymous contribution to *Open Hands*. These "bystanders" listen to verbal gay bashing and remain silent. They keep their feelings a secret and carry guilt privately.

2. Then there are the "perpetrators." They're not the Pat Robertsons of this era. *Closeted* "bystanders" sometimes turn into "perpetrators," too, becoming outspoken advocates of injustice itself! The Hebrew "taskmasters" enforced slavery upon their fellow Hebrews. They were rewarded for it, participating in the spoils of those who held the power, and we have similar "task masters" today. Recently several homophobic Anglican bishops in England admitted their previous gay relationships, in one case including prior arrest on public property. These are the folks who shout the loudest; taskmasters in our own denominations. In Norway they called them *Quislings*. In France, they were part of the Vichy government. In the Nuremberg trials, we called them traitors.

3. Another type is "the righteous Gentiles," who found every opportunity to resist the common assumptions and conversations that surrounded them. These are the gay and lesbian people who refuse to laugh at a joke at the expense of a gay, bisexual, or transgender person, even though laughing might be a kind of shield for their own identity. They are also the straight people who become articulate advocates for inclusiveness in the Church, though their behavior and point of view may contribute to the false impression that they, too, are gay. They are the ones who do not quickly add (or find ways to say), "But I'm not gay!" They find no need to "explain" themselves, and their solidarity is obvious.

4. The last choice might be called "rescuers." Here I want to address my comments particularly to the gays in this room and to those who also are in your families and among your friends.

We've already seen that "subversion" takes many forms. Pharaoh told the midwives to kill all Hebrew baby boys. Not only did they disregard what he said, but they also lied about it when he called them into his chambers. These midwives were skillful masters of deception and practitioners of innocence when it was necessary.

And in homes in Germany even youngsters learned to lie convincingly to authorities or feign innocence when caught. As Eva Fogelman tells it in her book, *Conscience and Courage*,[2] this was typical. One time hidden Jews had barely enough time to disappear into a hiding place when Nazis burst into the residence of their rescuers. In plain view was a table littered with cigarette butts and cards. Smoke still lingered in the air. But a German nine-year-old spoke up, confessing that he and his friends had been secretly playing cards and smoking. He pleaded with the soldiers not to tell his mother, as she would whip him if she knew. The soldiers promised to keep his secret and left. Resistance—and faithfulness—takes many forms.

You see, Truth may not always be what it appears to be. It is not always an absolute matter! Katie Cannon, womanist theologian, in writing about black women's lives in general, would support this nine-year-old rescuer. She says, "[It is necessary to] assert a human validity that is not derived from the white-male-norm . . . [We must explore] the relativity of truth and how to dispel the threat of death in order to seize life in the present . . . [the] moral quality of life [is] not an ideal, but [is] fulfilled as a balance of complexities in such a way that suffering does not overwhelm, and endurance with integrity [is] possible."[3]

"Seizing life in the present" also requires discernment of who has a "right" to hear the truth. That nine-year-old had the insight to determine that with the threat of death, endurance was the most moral response to the complexities of that situation. In the face of suffering, his response was, indeed, one of moral integrity.

In the Minnesota Conference some years ago, one of our deacons, Rick Huskey, came out to our then bishop. In the course of the conversation, he said, "You mean, bishop, that if I'm honest about who I am as a gay man with a call to ministry, I'm not fit for ministry, but if I lie about it, I am?" The bishop's response is unimportant, though the Board of Ministry did rule against Rick. Rick's personal response to his removal from ordained ministry was to remain faithful to his call by co-founding Affirmation, an organization for gay and lesbian United Methodists. Today Rick continues his ministry as a medical doctor who teaches geriatric medicine. His medical practice includes ministry to geriatric AIDS patients. That episode in Rick's life raises the question to all of us as to whether the Church always has a "right" to hear the truth.

So I'd like to come right out and say that there are times when lying, deception, and operating under false pretenses is the most *life-giving* action, the *most* faithful response for Christians. Of course, there is no point in defining these actions in a vacuum; what matters is the goal toward which an activity is directed. (In ethics that's a school of thought known as "consequentialism"; earlier Niebuhr emphasized consequences within an ethic of responsibility.) Or as John Howard Yoder puts it, "It's like the pressure of a fireman's hose. Aimed at a burning building, it is good; aimed at people marching in the street, it is bad." And he goes on to say "we must evaluate the worth of the value being violated; an unjust law or promise to do evil perhaps *should* be violated; the rights or integrity of a person or a community should *not*." Perhaps Augustine is saying, "Love God and sin boldly" to some gay and lesbian clergy when they deny their sexuality for the sake of their ministry. The Exodus passage says that the midwives did it because they feared God more than they feared unjust authority. The midwives lied, and the people of God were given their lives back again. And the other women in the story defied, were deceptive, and made false claims. Because of it the Hebrews were called out of exile, bound for the promised land.

Let me be clear that I believe there are many positions that gay and lesbian clergy can take about their sexual orientation. I have been profoundly moved, as I'm sure you have, by those who have come out, saying publicly that it is a matter of "integrity," that they can no longer "live a lie." We honor them for their choice, and it is only with sadness that we accept their decision that our denomination has no place for their ordained ministry. In some cases, they have become extremely effective pastors in other denominations, to the terrible loss of The United Methodist Church; in other cases they have been forced to turn their backs on their calling from God because the gate-keepers of the Church have refused to allow them to stay. There are some who have now chosen to fulfill their Christian voca-tion in other ways. (At this point in the sermon the congrega-tion is asked to speak names aloud as each of the following three questions are presented: Who are offering their gifts of ordained ministry in The United Methodist Church through another denomination? Who are the host of persons who are now clergy in the United Church of Christ instead of our own? Who would you add to the list?)

These, my friends, are the great company of witnesses, that surround us today, calling forth many of our best and brightest, those who have loved God, God's world, and this Church. They join us in "the Walk" today, searching for a place in a faith they cannot leave.

But not all of those who "come out" do so because they believe they have been living a lie. And not all gay and lesbian clergy need to. Moses had no trouble with *his* conscience— either for killing the Egyptian or for masquerading as an Egyptian himself. Rather, he knew that the time had come when a political statement had to be made by a confrontation, and he chose to assume personal responsibility for unjust authority. And so there are times when an action is necessary as a politi-cal act. And it is that choice I make today. I am one to tell you that a lesbian clergywoman can serve 37 years in this conference and in The United Methodist Church—faithfully, I believe.

I have been a lesbian all my life. My primary struggle took place in seminary, where, because of what I had learned in church, I was obsessed with seeking forgiveness and grace because of my sexual orientation. (One good result: I became a specialist in the book of Romans and neo-orthodox theology, both of which talk a lot about sin!) In my journey, certain friendships have grown into love relationships, and I rejoice in the gifts, over the years, they brought into my life. I was partnered for seventeen years, and divorce was as painful to me as it might be to anyone in this room. After seven years, I am still grieving that loss. Because I had no other family members when she left, I reached out for help, and other close friends—all church friends who named themselves "the family group"—surrounded me.

There are many, many people in our Church who know I am lesbian—but they don't ask and I don't have to tell! (In fact, when I told a few close friends what I was going to do in this sermon, they said, "Well, that won't be a surprise, will it?") I have not been unaware of bishops who have asked me in deeply moving ways how I was doing. I don't know how they and others like them knew, but I'm sure they did. Others with whom I have shared my stories up front simply chose not to tell anyone else. Underneath it all, you see, has been a daring to trust. I am confident that there are many United Methodists—in all arenas of the Church—who do not believe the "incompatibility" statement. And when you know people love and care for you, you can be confident that they can be "consequentialists," too. Without those folks, we would have had no bread for the journey.

Almost fifteen years ago one of those persons who enabled me to give thanks to God for the good gift of my sexuality confronted me with, "If I had to choose between the Church and my sexuality, I'd choose my sexuality every time!"

"Well, I wouldn't," I quickly replied. But I think her comment was the beginning of my journey to this moment. And in making this Walk, I am still choosing the Church because I want so much what Christ wants the Christian community to be: the banquet table, abundant with diversity and nurturing food; a table where invitations go out to everyone, coming together around the bread and wine offered to us by the Christ who is our Host.

I have chosen the Church before. When I withdrew from an almost certain episcopal election in 1976 because I did not want—as the first woman bishop, and for the sake of the Church—to have my life under a magnifying glass. I also knew, without my partner, I could not have the kind of life that I would need to sustain me through difficult times. From that moment on, I tried to open doors for other women, to raise the glass ceiling for women of color, to work behind the scenes for the election of other women to the episcopacy, and to be present to younger ordained women, because I had no women mentors to follow early in my ministry. Ultimately, I believe I chose "the better way."

Army Captain Lawrence Rockwood was recently court-martialed for personally investigating horrendous human rights abuses in Haiti against orders. He said that he was motivated by what his veteran father told him about the Dachau concentration camp: "The reason these things are created is because of blind obedience and cynicism." Now whether we're talking about the Holocaust, or the condition of prisons in Haiti, or the Church's position about gay and lesbian persons, there are choices to be made about how you're going to *be* in our Church. Resistance to blind obedience has many forms. And there are alternatives to cynicism. Staying in the Church does not always mean one's integrity is compromised, and actions of subversion, trust in the community of koinonia, and political action can provide abundant energy for living and serving.

I have chosen to swim against the stream in many areas of controversy, not because it's easy, but because I truly believe that the Church is the Body of Christ, called to share its message of healing, reconciliation, and yes, salvation. I do not choose the Church because I want simply to "belong," but because I believe in its transforming Spirit. I am confident that the Church is always renewing itself. And I will be there always seeking to be faithful to the One who has given it birth and continues to urge it into bringing wholeness and healing to the world. The midwives, the women of Moses' time, and Moses himself have led the way. And Christ makes that journey to the promised land with us. Perhaps you have read Alice Walker's book, *Possessing the Secret of Joy.* Do you remember what the secret was? Resistance! It's also the title of a poem by Connie Fife:

> resistance is a woman
> whose land is all on fire
> perseverance and determination
> are her daughters
> she is a Palestinian mother who
> hands her children a legacy of

war together with the
weapons to fight in it
she is a black woman draped
in purple satin who strolls
down a runway allowing only
the clothes she wears to be sold
resistance is the absent native woman
who died at the hands of
a white artist
who lives inside herself
while thriving inside of me
resistance is a girl child who
witnesses her mother's death and
swears to survive no matter
where the hiding place
she is a woman beaten with hate
by the man she loves who
decides to escape to a world
where touch is sacred
resistance is a woman who defies
the male definition of love
and loves another woman
then heals an entire nation in doing so
she is a woman torn apart by
the barbed wire surrounding her home
who plots a way out
despite the consequences
resistance is every woman who
has ever considered taking up
arms writing a story leaving the abuse
saving her children or saving herself
she is every woman who dares
to stage a revolution complete a novel
be loved or change the world
resistance walks across a landscape
of fire accompanied by her daughters
perseverance and determination[4]

It may be a landscape of fire, but oh, what a journey!

Notes

1. This is the title of a book by A. Roy Eckardt. *A Long Night's Journey into Day* (Detroit: Wayne State University Press, 1982).

2. Eva Fogelman, *Conscience and Courage* (New York: Anchor Books, 1994).

3. Katie G. Cannon, *Black Womanist Ethics* (Atlanta: Scholars Press, 1988).

4. Connie Fife, "Resistance," from *The Colour of Resistance: A Contemporary Collection of Writing by Aboriginal Women,* ed. Connie Fife (Toronto: Sister Vision Press, 1993). Used by permission.

Chapter 8

Barbara B. Troxell

Resisting the Church on Homosexuality

As a lifelong Methodist and then United Methodist, I love this denomination at the same time that I have serious disagreements with it. As an institution we have become so institution-protective and culture-bound that we are in danger of losing touch with the Spirit of God who is the ground of our being and the stimulus for all our actions of love and justice. Most particularly I am in strong disagreement with our various Disciplinary statements against gay and lesbian persons. These statements are eminently unjust, incredibly cruel, and deeply harmful not only to gay, lesbian, and bisexual persons but to all United Methodists. The *Discipline* statement about "the practice of homosexuality" being "incompatible with Christian teaching" assumes that we humans are primarily *doing* creatures rather than *being* creatures. This is manifestly unfair and, in fact, untrue to the biblical witness of God's grace-filled creating of us all in God's own image.

I have served as an ordained minister for forty years—as a parish pastor in three different settings, as a campus minister and student YWCA director in two universities, as a conference council director and then district superintendent, as a seminary dean of students, and currently, for nearly eleven years, on faculty of a United Methodist theological seminary. In these vari-

122

ous settings, I have witnessed the anguish among diverse persons, regardless of their orientation, caused by the denominational proscriptions against gay and lesbian persons. My resistance to the anti-gay statements in our United Methodist *Book of Discipline* has taken many forms: pastoral conversations with lesbian, gay, and bisexual candidates for ministry; accompaniment of candidates under duress; verbal and written support of bishops and other public authority figures who have stood strongly against the denominational proscriptions; clearly articulated stands in my teaching, preaching, pastoral care, and superintending ministries against such injustice noting where I differ with denominational positions. I'd like to describe some of these in more detail.

Pastoral conversations with lesbian, gay, and bisexual candidates. Both as a superintendent and as a seminary dean of students and faculty member in two diverse theological schools, I have been available to students who were candidates for ordination. Persons have sought me out to consult about how they, who knew themselves to be lesbian or gay *and* to be called by God to ordained ministry, would maneuver through the minefields of the district committee and conference board of ordained ministry interviews. As a member of a board of ordained ministry in earlier years, I know well the importance of thorough, careful, and wise interviewing of candidates. I know that some who feel personally called by God may not yet be ready in their process for the confirming of their call by the larger community of faith. But to be denied candidacy on the basis of sexual orientation is neither fair nor just. So, with applicants for ordination, I have listened with care, we have reviewed the *Discipline*, we have strategized together, and we have prayed together for the candidate and for more openness within The United Methodist Church. There is real agony here, as candidates must move through the process, seeking to be true to their own integrity, yet unable to share with the interviewing committees one of the most important aspects of their beings. Too often, they are asked by the Church to withhold the truth, evade the question, or lie directly, to protect their sense of call to ordained ministry.

Accompaniment of candidates under duress. Some incidents of accompaniment have occurred when boards of ordained ministry have heard rumors about the alleged sexual orientation of candidates and wish to check these with the candidates. I have accompanied persons to these meetings as a mentor and adviser so that there is support, as the allegations are presented, the facts clarified, and the situation reviewed.

Support of bishops and other public authority figures who stand in opposition to the anti-gay proscriptions. Orally and in writing I have been supportive of bishops, such as the "Denver 15,"[1] who have stated clearly their opposition to the anti-gay statements in *The Book of Discipline*. Many of these bishops are friends whom I have known through the years, prior to their election to the episcopacy. Their witness has inspired us and continues to strengthen us for deeper justice and love within the Christian community and the larger world. These bishops and many district superintendents and board of ordained ministry members find themselves in the position of having to say, in effect, to their clergy colleagues and candidates, "Please don't tell me about your sexual orientation; and I will not ask." We are caught, as a church, in the "don't ask, don't tell" mode, made famous by the United States military establishment around this same issue. I stand solidly with these colleagues who are in more public positions of authority than I am, and who sadly find their own integrity violated by unjust rules of the denomination.

Clear stands in my teaching, preaching, superintending ministries against unjust stands against lesbian, gay, bisexual persons. Students know where I personally stand on these issues, for I say it clearly. Even when I teach the course in Twentieth Century United Methodist Studies, and seek to present the diverse points of view in the denomination around homosexuality, I consider it essential that the class know where I stand. I indicate that I am open to dialogue and to hearing the opposing point of view. But I must be true to who I am in stating my disagreement with and resistance to the statements in *The Book of Discipline* on this issue.

My resistance to the denominational proscriptions against

lesbian, gay, and bisexual persons arises from several sources. First, I believe that all of us are created in the image of God, and that God does not make anyone evil or even "incompatible with Christian teaching." I believe that sexual orientation is a good gift of God; the choice we have is how we relate with integrity to ourselves and one another and all of creation through our sexual orientation—whether we are same-gendered or other-gendered in our orientation. If we are forced to be untrue to ourselves, we will tend to be untrue and perhaps abusive to others and to all of creation.

Second, I believe that whenever a group of persons in their being or their behavior is named "incompatible" there is gross injustice. We have had such naming in relation to persons of color; eventually we learned that such naming was racist and utterly unjust. We have had such naming in relation to women; eventually we learned that such naming was sexist and utterly unjust. We have had such naming in relation to the poor (and others in the so-called "working class"); we learned that such naming was classist and utterly unjust. We have had such naming in relation to the physically, mentally, and emotionally handicapped; eventually we learned that such naming was utterly unjust. In the many generations where racism, sexism, classism, and handicappism have been rampant, we have recognized that unjust naming led to violence against persons of color and women, against the poor and the differently abled. This is what we are seeing much more visibly now against gay, lesbian, bisexual, and transgendered persons.

Third, Jesus Christ lived and preached the gracious reign of God for all persons. Jesus apparently said nothing about homosexual persons, but he said much about persons who righteously sought to fence the reign of God only for persons like themselves. Can we do any less or any more? As we seek to be the people of God and the hands and feet of Christ in our day, we must resist all efforts to close off the reign of God. To use another image, the welcome table of Christ must be hospitably open to all. We clergy who are celebrants at that table are most guilty when we fence it in, and call anyone incompatible to come to it with all their gifts and their wounds.

I am aware that my "loyal opposition" and "resistance," so far, have been primarily in behind-the-scenes actions. This way seems to be my calling, rather than in public pronouncements or in headline-making news. I wonder sometimes if I am fearful of too much publicity; perhaps it might be. But as more of an introvert than an extrovert, the way I have been led has been through pastoral conversations, personal support, and stands through teaching, preaching, and now writing. Who knows where God will lead next?

Note

1. The Denver 15 is a group of fifteen bishops who, at the 1996 General Conference in Denver, wrote and signed a letter opposing The United Methodist Church's proscriptive language against gay and lesbian persons within the Church.

Chapter 9

Susan Laurie

That's the Dumbest Thing I've Ever Heard!

A Sermon on Resisting Invisibility[1]
Text: Psalm 31

The lectionary reading today is from the book of Psalms. I want you to know that this is the Psalm that God led me to when I was beginning to understand myself as both a Christian and a lesbian—at a time when the pieces of my life were finally coming together.

The great thing about this Psalm is that the author, the "prayer," lets it all out. No emotion is hidden. All the joys, all the burdens are expressed in depth. Every part of the self, the whole person, is shared with God. What I discovered in this, is that the feelings that I could not express, I found articulated for me in this passage. Somehow, that long ago person spoke my feelings.

Although this is one of my favorite Psalms, I sometimes hesitate to tell people that because in the middle there is a chunk that sounds seriously paranoid. But now, I claim that part too, because I have learned that when people are *really* out to get you, it is not paranoia.

I resonate with the psalmist. I would like to share the entire psalm and invite you to listen as a whole person. And whatever thoughts you bring to worship today—be bold, name God, voice your complaint as loudly as your praise, and trust your most authentic self to God.

Read Psalm 31 aloud and slowly.

Today I have more of a testimony than a sermon, and I realize that it may mean more to me than to you. And whatever worth you may find in my words, it is a result of God's love and presence in my life.

I have been myself for as long as I can remember. It's true. I have been myself for as long as I can remember. And very early in life my little self went to Sunday school. I sang "Jesus loves me this I know for the Bible tells me so," and I believed it. I learned about Jesus and I learned that I am a person of worth, receiving love and care from God. I learned that as a Christian I could pass on the light and love of God. I sang, "This little light of mine, I'm gonna let it shine! Hide it under a bushel? NO! I'm gonna let it shine."

I was blessed with Sunday school teachers, choir directors, and grandparents who got the lesson inside of me. It could not get out. It was part of me. I was a Christian.

Of course, this does not mean that I was always well behaved. Oh no, Christian perfection was not at work here. I was mean and rotten in between moments of good. I was from a family of eight children and there was plenty of childish nastiness to go around. My brother Bob was my usual cohort—we were close in age. We had a bunch of little brothers and sisters, and we just didn't want them playing with us all of the time. They bothered us, slowed us down. Often we told them to get lost.

One day, however, that was not the case. Bob and I decided to play a board game. I don't remember if it was *Sorry* or *Trouble*—but we were both. We got the game out. Our little brother, Scott, who was five or six at the time, was playing with his little cars beside the couch minding his own business—you know those Hot Wheels cars with the looping track. *He* wasn't bothering us, but Bob and I started teasing him.

I said, loud enough for Scott to hear, "Too bad Scott is not here, we'd like to have a third person to play this game with us." Scott perked his head up from behind the couch and said, "Hey, I'm right here."

We really had not planned it, but Bob joined right in with me, "Yeah, too bad Scott's not here."

"Scott, Scott, where *are* you?"

"Here I am. I'm right here. I will play!" Scott came running over. He was excited to be included for a change.

But we completely ignored him. We kept on hollering, "SCOTT! We need another player. . . . Where aaaare you?"

"I'm here! I want to play!" But we continued to deny his presence.

"Oh well, let's just start playing without him."

Scott, frustrated to come so close to being included and then be shut out, went out to the kitchen to my mother and appealed to her. "Mom, Bob and Sue won't let me play with them. They say I'm not here."

Mom replied, "Don't be silly, of course you're here."

"They are out there and they say I am not here!" He was close to tears.

You know, Bob and I really got into that power. We were having so much fun we even called out to the kitchen, "Mom, have you seen Scott? We want him to play a game." Well, she called us out, and we were so bold we asked her again, while Scott was standing right beside her, "We are looking for Scott, we thought he would want to play. Have you seen him?"

Mom gave Bob and me *the look*. "You two stop it and let him play." We left the kitchen, smug as before—insiders.

Scott had to stay another minute because he was crying by now and still saying, "They say I'm not here!" Mom looked at him and said, "Scott, that's the dumbest thing I've ever heard. After all, here is your arm and I can hear you talking. Of course you are here. Don't let them do that to you. Now you go out there and play."

We finally stopped teasing him, but it amazes me even now how dynamic that was. I felt guilty about it, but it seemed worth it. Scott had been happily playing with his Hot Wheels cars and we just pretended he was invisible and reduced him to tears in minutes. What power!

Scott made an appeal to my mother. That was good—she could fix it. But why did we do it to him? Why did we pick *him*? Well, practically speaking, it wouldn't have worked on our older brothers; they would have told us to scram. It would only work on someone weaker and unsure of himself.

I think of that story as I search for a way to share my experience as a young adult in The United Methodist Church. I was 26 years old and single. I had been active in church all of my life—an insider, a player. But for the first time I was also admitting to myself that I was homosexual in sexual/affectional orientation. And from the time when I had experienced my first "crushes," I also knew to keep my feelings to myself. I had kept my identity secret and separate from my church life. As I was finally working to understand my sexual orientation and what that meant for me, I also heard a cultural voice saying to me, "Sue, you cannot be gay and Christian. That does not exist." It was telling me, "I am not here."

Homosexuality was not addressed directly in my local church, but through the silence I got the message that I should not talk about it either. However, there were other groups who were saying it aloud. "Homosexuality is incompatible with Christian teaching" was and still is the mantra of The United Methodist Church.

I was single and lonely at that time—unsure of myself, vulnerable to that message. It had power over me. So I denounced my homosexuality and became more "Christian" in the culturally approved sense. How? Simple. There were always people willing to explain their superiority and I listened to their formula: I became more active in my United Methodist church; I joined a weekly Bible study; sang in the choir; went to Sunday school; gave an offering; never missed worship. I told my old friends—you know, the riffraff gay and lesbian friends who'd always supported me—that I could not hang out with them anymore. They were a temptation to me, and so I dismissed them. I confessed my orientation to two or three other Christians who I knew hated homosexuality. I told them so they would "hold me accountable." And I prayed to God. I was faithful and full of repentance. I asked God to change me.

I started reading scripture, and I got really holy. Matthew through Acts—I read strai . . . right through. (Sorry, I almost said "straight." I had always read it straight before. That was the problem!) I thought the Gospels were a good place to start. The Bible lay open on my kitchen table. I read it every day.

I read it a little bit at a time. Partly, I was afraid. I had never read it start to finish, and I was afraid that every next page was going to condemn me by slamming my orientation. I tried to be ready for the rejection of God.

Slowly, transformation started to happen, but not the one I'd been praying for. There were the stories I knew: Jesus and the miracles; Jesus loving the outcasts; Jesus who said, "let the little children come to me"; the parable of the lost sheep. Miss Reed had taught me about the shepherd who had one hundred sheep, but when ninety-nine returned and one was lost, that shepherd would leave the ninety-nine to go find the one that was lost. So precious are we to God, God will not let us go. I read those stories and I was reminded of God's love for me.

Meanwhile, I had to live out the other parts of my life. Part of the invisibility was performing as if nothing was bothering me. I taught high school, and I coached. I had new friends, but they did not know me. My old friends gave me space. They were hurt by my rejection but kind enough to stand by me. Weeks turned into months.

I diligently read on. By the time I got to the Gospel of John, I was really conflicted. I had not yet seen a reference that denounced me, not a word that rejected me, and nothing about what a horrible, unredeemable sinner I was. I saw nothing that called me to confess my "sin." Instead, what was written over and over again was that Jesus claimed me.

John 10:27 quotes Jesus, "My sheep hear my voice. I know them, and they follow me. I give them eternal life, and they will never perish. No one will snatch them out of my hand." Thank you, Jesus.

I kept reading, and I kept feeling the affirmation of God who loves me. But this only caused greater confusion. I had tried so hard to renounce my orientation, to hate that part of myself, to get rid of it, to integrate the Church's hate for homosexuality into my soul. But it was Christ and the gospel that did not allow me to fragment. Jesus was not letting me go.

I was so confused. Previously I had kept my sexuality and Christianity separate from each other—separate compartments of my being—now I thought I was dealing with it.

Worship started to be a problem. I did not feel real. I could fool people, but not myself. I knew I was still the same. I tried to worship and hide at the same time. I would not bring my whole self to the liturgy—just the accepted part. I would pray, but I would deny my hurt. I believe now that God kept after me through the grace that was preached every week. However, at that time I felt the real me was invisible to the preacher and the rest of the congregation. My battle for acceptance was harsh. I had my new friends there, but they did not know my struggle. Even if they did, I knew they would only be interested in change, not in acceptance.

I was trying harder and harder to overcome my homosexuality. I imagined myself heterosexual—married to a man, kids—but the picture didn't work. Strangely, I began to feel more distant from God even though my appearance and effort were so faithful. For all of my activity, my connection to God was diminishing. I was disappearing.

I could not talk about this to any friends. The riffraff had been dismissed, and the people at the church hated my homosexuality. A few perceived the surface of my hurt and offered, "No pain, no gain." So I took on the pain as necessary. I felt I was created outside of God's intention. I was damaged, worth less to God because I was gay. I was unable to fix myself, and God was uninterested in fixing me.

I kept up my outward Christian appearance, but I could not pretend to myself that God was fooled by my "changes." *The Book of Discipline* is clear that you cannot be homosexual and Christian. Since I could not deny the one maybe I had to deny the other. The next logical conclusion was that I would have to stop being Christian.

I became very sad. I did not want to give up Jesus. I did not want to lose the shepherd who would not lose me. I needed my connection to God, it was a part of me to live in the hope of Jesus Christ. I believed in him. I had felt the Spirit, at least before this "I'm not gay" charade began. Who would I be without God or the Church in my life? Anguish. Torment. Separation. Sadness. "Sue, where aaaare you?" They say I'm not here.

But I was blessed, and I still had not depleted the good foundation of faith I had integrated as a child. Finally in my frustration I cried out to God—authentically. I remember that I was in my apartment, in tears, and I formed the words—actually spoke them out loud:

> Why did you do this to me? Is it a test?
> I know I am not straight.
> Why did you make me this way?
> Do you think this is funny? You know I'm gay.
> Why did you make me gay and then forbid it?
> I don't want to be alone, always.
> Am I a joke to you?
> Are you sitting up there laughing at me?

I had cried out loud, "Are you laughing at me, a gay Christian?" Then God spoke, "That is the dumbest thing I've ever heard!"

You know, we need the vernacular when we get too holy. And as honest as I am standing here, these are the words I heard from God: "That is the dumbest thing you have ever said, Sue. I love you, you have known this all of your life. The Scriptures reminded you when you looked, how did you get off track?"

"Well, people say gay Christians do not exist. They say I am not here."

"Of course they exist, you are right here. Don't be silly. Here is your arm. I can hear your voice. Now go back in there. Don't let them do that to you."

God was speaking to someone who had cloaked herself in all this holiness and righteous appearance, but underneath there was a learned self-hate and homophobia, and finally a core of tremendous vulnerability and pain.

God's voice cut through all of that. And I started to heal. For a while the healing was just between God and me. Because where else could I go?

One day I went to the church where I grew up. I entered the sanctuary and approached the communion table which held a large Bible. And I don't know what kind of theology permits this or bans it, but I thought, "God, just this one time, could you help me out? I need a verse!"—and I let the Bible fall open. The pages revealed Psalms 30 and 31.

Psalm 30 is wonderful: "weeping may [last] for the night, but joy comes [in] the morning" (verse 5).

But it was Psalm 31 that spoke for me. I could only think, "God, I don't know what to pray, I don't know what to say, I trust you, but it is so lonely here." And there was Psalm 31, saying for me:

> In you, O Lord, I seek refuge; do not let me ever be put to shame; in your righteousness deliver me. . . . You are indeed my rock and my fortress; for your name's sake lead me and guide me, take me out of the net that is hidden for me, for you are my refuge. Into your hand I commit my spirit; you have redeemed me, O Lord, faithful God. (verses 1-5)

My feelings surfaced. The pain, which was so deep that I could not describe it, was there articulated for me.

I prayed, "Be gracious to me, O Lord, for I am in distress; my eye wastes away from grief, my soul and body also . . . I have passed out of mind like one who is dead; I have become a broken vessel."

It was all there—even the part where I could admit that I had enemies and they were after me and I wanted something to happen to them, "Let the lying lips be stilled."

The psalmist lets it all come out. And there also is the hope. God is present, God is steadfast in love—"I had said in my alarm, 'I am driven far from your sight.' But you heard my supplications when I cried out to you for help."

My sincere attempt to stop being lesbian had been tearing me apart. My relationship with God was tearing as well and I did not know why. But I know why now. I could no longer feel God's grace because I had been trying to *earn* it. I would "do all things" and prove myself worthy. I was going to do the work of Jesus and earn my own salvation. That is why the distance between God and me had grown so great.

God's grace is a gift. In trying to justify myself, I was losing Christ. Campus Crusade for Christ has a definition for sin that I knew then and still like now: sin is anything that separates one from God. In my efforts to change, I had never felt so separate from God, and now I name what I was doing as sin.

I still hear people say homosexual Christians do not exist. But as my brother Scott had insisted, "I am right here!" I admit that sometimes they get to me. I whine and complain. You have seen me do it. I get frustrated and jump up and down crying, "They're saying that I don't exist!" But here I am. When others flex their power and continue to play their game, they ignore the presence of many, many, many faithful, unnamed faithful, people who serve God.

My healing continues. At times, I still suffer from my own homophobia. For example, when I am invited to preach at different places, where most times my orientation does not come up, I do my prayer, and I offer my sermon. But after the benediction, when people would tell me I did a nice job, in my head I would sometimes think, "Well, if they knew who I was, then they would not say that." This is my own homophobia undermining my wholeness. Fear of being gay permeates this culture and I catch myself perpetuating it. I want to confess that. And I repent of it. After all, being lesbian is God's blessing. My insights and preaching are informed by the blessings I have received.

I cannot ignore what God has done for me. So I give a testimony.

My testimony is that I find solace with Jesus, and I hug the stories of the faith. I love God, who will call me back when I feel rejected. In spite of the efforts of The United Methodist Church, both covert and overt, I am a whole person. Whether or not I struggle within The United Methodist Church or disappear from its brokenness, I am thankful for my wholeness.

My faith and my hope are in Jesus the Christ. He is my Savior, my Lord, my companion. In John 15, Jesus calls me friend and tells me to abide in his love.

I know that others are uncomfortable to know a gay Christian, so they denounce me in order to be comfortable again—my "dis-integration" for their comfort. I tell Jesus that the pain I experience is so real, that I feel like I am being torn in half.

Jesus says, "I know."

When others say, "Just don't tell anyone that you are a homosexual," I remember when Jesus came to me and said, "I knew you before you did and I blessed you. Have faith, trust in me." And so I do.

When I am pushed to justify myself, I relax for Jesus is my justification.

Psalm 31 says:

> In you, O LORD, I seek refuge; . . .
> I will exult and rejoice in your steadfast love,
>   because you have seen my affliction;
>   you have taken heed of my adversities,
> and have not delivered me into the hand of the enemy;
>   you have set my feet in a broad place. (verses 1, 7-8)

"God is our refuge. And our strength. A present help in time of trouble. We will not fear."[2] Amen.

(Author's note: Communion was celebrated at the service in which this sermon was preached. The liturgy was taken from *We Were Baptized Too*, Marilyn Bennett Alexander and James Preston [Louisville: Westminster John Knox Press, 1996].)

Notes

1. This sermon was originally given on March 18, 1997 in the Chapel of the Unnamed Faithful, Garrett-Evangelical Theological Seminary, Evanston, Illinois.

2. Actual text from that day's anthem sung by the G-ETS choir.

Chapter 10

Terry L. Norman

A Journey Toward Authenticity

Take thou authority to preach the gospel!" Those were the words boldly proclaimed by Missouri Bishop Eugene M. Frank as I knelt before him in the chancel of Linn Memorial Church in Fayette. As he and other elders placed hands on my head as an act of ordination, the words spoken there branded themselves into my soul as nothing else ever had.

All this was thirty years ago, but I remember it as if it were yesterday. I had just graduated from Saint Paul School of Theology in Kansas City. Like 95 percent of seminary students in the late 1960s, I was white, male, and assumed by the Church to be straight. And I considered myself straight, believing that the sexual attraction I occasionally experienced for other men would become a thing of the past once I "married the right woman." After all, that was the unquestioned "wisdom" of the day.

Bishop Frank chose Missouri's capital as my first appointment, sending me to Wesley Church in Jefferson City. It was a young congregation less than a year old, and with that appointment eventually came all the success I had been programmed to achieve. During that first year at Wesley I married a wonderful young woman, and as time passed God blessed us with the birth of two sons and a daughter.

Life within our all-American family was not as the outside world assumed it to be, however. Following the birth of our second child, the depression I felt deep inside had become apparent to my wife, Mary. She knew something was badly wrong and demanded an explanation.

"Are you involved with another woman?" she asked. "If you are, tell me. Something has caused you to lose interest in our relationship and I want to know what."

To the best of my recollection, I finally managed to say something like, "No . . . I'm not involved with anyone . . . but if I were . . . it probably wouldn't be . . . with . . . a woman." I thought the world would end that moment.

But our world didn't end. Instead, we talked for hours and I explained that I had gradually come to think of myself as "bisexual," the term that seemed best to describe the experience I had of myself in those days. I recall characterizing myself as "80 percent straight," and assuring Mary that I could handle whatever the future proved the other 20 percent to be. I recall saying something like, "I have no intention of allowing my interest in men to sabotage our marriage, and I could never, ever adopt a gay lifestyle."

Somehow I knew that wasn't the whole truth, though. I knew there were parts of myself either undiscovered or long-lost to conscious memory. "Authenticity" was a word that belonged in the dictionary and seemed to have little relevance for the life I lived. "Congruence," that is, to know oneself and to live consistently therewith, was a concept that seemed beyond my grasp. I was a role player, a "false self" living out a life script written by the culture around me. I experienced myself as emotionally blind in so many ways, like one groping in the darkness in search of the "true self" that God had created. In pain and confusion, I clung to my faith like a drowning man to a life preserver. And nothing in the gospel I had been ordained to preach seemed quite as important as the words of Jesus concerning truth—he promised that it had the power to set us free!

The wisdom of the gospel that encouraged me to seek the truth about myself eventually led to two graduate degrees in counseling and an emotional roller-coaster ride that almost took my life. As that ride neared its end after two long decades, the person I discovered was not the individual I had always believed myself to be, not the person I had been told by my Church and society I should be, and certainly not the person I wanted to be. I discovered there a gay married man with three children, a "pseudo-heterosexual" who had faked straight so well for so long that he had fooled even himself most of the time. I discovered that I had been systematically repressing my same-gender orientation since the onset of adolescence. All that time I had little or no idea that the direction of my deepest need for physical, emotional, and spiritual love was toward a person like myself—toward another man.

Naively, I had always assumed that orientation was about sexual behavior, and I had been highly successful at *behaving* heterosexually. I had married, fathered children, and complied with all the gender role expectations demanded of a straight male. I had suppressed my inclination toward homosexual behavior with equal success, only to discover eventually that orientation was not about sex at all. Rather, my same-gender orientation proved to be about my innate need to love and be loved by another man in a committed, ongoing relationship.

Yes, finally, I realized that orientation was *a matter of love*, not sex, and that behaving heterosexually in marriage no more makes a gay man straight than behaving homosexually in prison makes a straight man gay.

As shocking as the discovery of my same-gender orientation might have been, that was nothing compared to the realization that I had come to sanity as the result of a lifelong struggle with God. While I was doing all I could to deny the truth about myself, God was doing all God could to help me grasp and appreciate the beauty of my gay soul.

It is impossible to describe fully what a wrestling match with God feels like, especially when it occurs across the course of one's entire adulthood. All I can tell you is that my ego strength was not sufficient to sustain the struggle against God's creative spirit. Gradually, I came to know and accept the truth: that I was a gay man through and through; that God had created me that way; that I was fully acceptable to my creator, regardless of the Church's position to the contrary; and that there was nothing incompatible between my same-gender orientation and the gospel I had been ordained to preach!

With the passing of time, God's gracious gift of unconditional loving acceptance even persuaded me to finally begin loving myself. The sense of inferiority, of sinfulness and guilt, which had always plagued my life, gave way to an awesome sense of self-acceptance. The pain of internalized homophobia faded away as I experienced my own Golgotha—old beliefs died, and I felt myself resurrected to a new life of optimism and hope.

So now that I knew myself as the gay man I was, now that I loved and accepted myself as the very man God had created, why did I set out systematically to destroy myself? The fact is, all my new realizations brought with them a depression more severe than any I had ever known. Yes, the truth had set my soul free from the lies that had enslaved me, yet all that internal change seemed to mean nothing in terms of my external world. I was still "the Reverend Dr. Norman," a married man with three children who had lived in the same community of fifty thousand for twenty years. During that time, I served on the Board of Ordained Ministry under two different bishops, pastored two of the county's three Methodist congregations, directed a Methodist-related counseling center, and even served two terms as president of the local ministerial alliance. I knew I had the love and respect of my church, my community, and my family. I felt all that would be destroyed if the truth were ever known.

So why was I depressed? I felt trapped. I saw no way out of my dilemma in this lifetime. Responsibility seemed to mandate keeping my mouth shut and carrying on the charade at which I was so well practiced.

The sheer physical cost of that charade eventually proved too much for my body, however. In addition to sleeping more and more, I stopped exercising, ate and drank far too much, and watched my normal thirty-two-inch waist creep up to a full forty-two inches. As I stepped onto a scale the morning of my forty-seventh birthday, it reflected an astonishing two hundred and thirty pounds. That's an enormous amount of weight for a five-foot, eight-inch frame. As I swallowed down my medications for hypertension and arrhythmia, I realized I could not go on this way. I saw a walking dead man in the bathroom mirror that morning, one well on his way to a premature grave. I knew something had to change—and now. The secret I had kept so well for so long was *literally* destroying me.

As the winter of 1990 gave way to the warmth of spring, I spent night after night walking the country road that meandered through the river valley near our home. The spiritual pain was excruciating, for I found myself accompanied by a God who insisted I could only save myself and the people I loved by telling the truth. God insisted that I "had to be Terry," and that "no new charade would do."

Yes, I felt urged by God to come out fully to my family and friends, but how could I possibly trust such a prehension? And what possible good could come from voluntary disclosure? I found the whole situation utterly baffling. Fear and self-doubt prevailed all summer, but by early fall I simply had no strength left with which to resist. Seeing no victory possible other than surrender, I began the painful task of disclosing my same-gender orientation to those persons whom I felt had a right to know—my immediate family, my colleagues at the counseling center, a few of my long-term clients, and numerous close friends.

Once the process got underway, I found it remarkably easy to come out privately to those persons who I knew loved me. Full *public* disclosure was quite a different matter, however, and certainly nothing I ever intended.

In retrospect, it's really clear that I attempted to take the coward's way out, particularly where the Church was concerned. From my years on the Board of Ordained Ministry, I knew full well the actual truth by which the Church lived when it came to same-gender orientation. We practiced an unspoken "don't ask, don't tell" policy long before that concept was adopted by the Pentagon. Gay and lesbian clergy were tolerated as long as they remained quietly in the closet, as long as they didn't become "self-avowed, practicing homosexuals."

Hiding behind that policy, I requested early retirement from parish ministry without disclosing my true orientation. I had every intention of devoting myself full time to the practice of professional counseling and never confronting United Methodism on its position concerning homosexuality.

And I might have done exactly that—abdicated my authority to preach the gospel and slipped away quietly—had it not been for the depressive episode of a young pastor named John Rice. He made an appointment at the counseling center where I worked at the urging of his superintendent, and the story that unfolded tore my closet door off its hinges. John has agreed to write that story for inclusion in this chapter, and I would like you to hear it in his own words:

> When I saw Jim lying dead in his bedroom that October morning, my first sense was relief that he had not shot himself in the head. He lay on his back within a shroud of acrid smoke, his eyes closed across his gray face, a quarter-sized circle of red staining the front of his flannel shirt. Jim had shot himself in the heart.
>
> He was alive when I first saw him earlier that day in the living room of the small frame house that belonged to his Aunt Mary. She had called and asked that I come speak with Jim. "He's in a terrible state of mind," she said. "He called the sheriff and asked for someone to drive him to the state mental hospital in Fulton."
>
> Jim sat on the couch opposite my chair, leaning forward, with hands clenched between his knees. Tight-jawed, teeth together, he forced the answer to my question, "What's the matter?"
>
> "I think . . . I'm . . . a damn queer . . . and I'm afraid the men of the church know about me."
>
> That was the first and last statement of self-disclosure Jim made to any of us who shared life with him in the small United Methodist congregation in California, Missouri. During my four-year pastorate there, I had never known Jim to instigate conversation with anyone, except on Sunday mornings when he greeted us with an economy of words as we entered the sanctuary for worship. Jim was head usher, and kept a folding chair by the

door to the foyer. He sat quietly in that chair Sunday after Sunday, moving among the congregation only to take up the offering.

To the best of my knowledge, Jim had no social contacts other than the church and seeing to the needs of his elderly aunt. He was such a quiet man, and only 54 years old when he died.

I know I listened to his revelation with compassion and that my instinct was to be helpful. I think, though, that I was not helpful at all. I gave in to a contradictory instinct to flee the scene of his painful self-effacement. I told Jim I'd take him to the hospital, then left to inform the sheriff of our agreement. I couldn't wait to get out of there. Sadly, I would never speak with Jim again.

The phone rang as I sat in Sheriff Kenny Jones's office discussing Jim's situation. He answered, and his eyes grew wide as if he could see what he was hearing from Mary. Kenny put the receiver back into the cradle, guiding its descent with peripheral vision as he focused his eyes on me and said, "Jim just shot himself."

Kenny cut the typical five-minute travel time in half as we rode together in the county's Crown Victoria to Mary's house. We entered without knocking. Mary stood in the middle of the living room, biting her lower lip and pointing with a wavering left hand toward a hall leading into the bedroom.

Light poured into the hall through an east-facing window and diffused in gray rays through wisps of low-lying smoke drifting from the bedroom. I hesitated, meaning to let Kenny lead the way, as I supposed the sheriff should. But Kenny was hesitating, too, and it occurred to me that he was as reticent as I to see what we both feared. So I waded into the smoke first and passed across the threshold of the bedroom.

Mary fixed coffee for me while Kenny and the county coroner did their work in the bedroom. When they left with Jim's body, Mary asked me to look in the bedroom to make sure everything had been put in order.

I found there a small bloodstain on the braided throw rug upon which Jim had fallen to rest. I rolled the rug up and tucked it under my arm, intending to dispose of it later. As I looked around one last time before leaving, I noticed a gray mark on the floral wallpaper, and another like it on the ceiling. Suddenly, I realized what it was. I followed an imagined trajectory back to the door . . . and there . . . on the hardwood floor . . . lay the bullet that killed Jim!

I remember picking it up, holding it in the cup of my hand. It was dark and heavy, small but lethal, distorted by the impacts that had spent its energy. I dropped the bullet into my pocket and left the room. There was no more I could do.

Two days later John conducted Jim's funeral. He did his best to console Aunt Mary in the weeks that followed, and tried to help the congregation with its grief work. But the process was cut short by the holidays, by other deaths in the congregation, and by the pervasive desire on everyone's part to put the whole sordid matter behind them.

A full year passed before the severely depressed young pastor found his way into my counseling office. He spoke of being "fed up with ministry," and with "life in general." He said he felt "so unhappy," and "guilty for keeping his family in tears."

"Terry," he said, "I have everything a guy could want, so why am I having these feelings of gloom and despair? I have no energy or enthusiasm, and recently I have been taking over-the-counter meds just to sleep. I just wonder what happened along the way. Why did life lose its . . . well . . . whatever?"

John and I had been seeing one another weekly for over a month before Jim's name was finally mentioned. As the story began to unfold, John broke into tears, shook, and told me how guilty he felt for having "failed Jim."

"Terry, I saw him five minutes before and five minutes after he shot himself. I felt so badly about being that close . . . *that* close. Why didn't I do something different? People kept telling me not to blame myself, but I felt something go out of me as a result of what happened. I was his pastor, for God's sake! He was on the edge and I was within arm's length, but I missed it."

I sat quietly for a long time, just trying to absorb what I'd heard. Finally, John asked, "Do you think this has anything to do with the way I've been feeling? I've tried to put Jim out of my mind, and I never talk about what happened. Do you think . . . think . . . Jim can help me?"

There was no doubt in my mind that Jim could help, and that John had identified the source of his own depression. As we continued to talk, it became obvious that he had invested enormous energy in suppressing the tragedy of Jim's suicide. As a result, John had lost faith in himself as a person, a pastor, a husband, and father.

I'll never forget John saying, "How could I possibly graduate number one in my class at Iliff and still fail so badly? I should have stayed with UPS and spent my life delivering packages. Maybe I'll go back there, to UPS I mean, where I don't have to work with people."

Not only was John considering dropping out of pastoral ministry as a result of his perceived inadequacies, he also believed he was failing his wife and two children. "I'm afraid our marriage is on the rocks," he said. "Sometimes I feel as if they would all be better off without me."

As I listened to John's story unfold, *I realized that the bullet which passed through Jim had struck his young pastor as well.* Its impact had inflicted life-threatening depression. As a direct result of Jim's suicide, the Church almost lost one of its finest ministers, and Kathy and the children could have easily lost the husband and father they loved.

Thankfully, John recovered across time. My own anger turned to rage, though, as I began to realize how many other "Jims" and "Johns" filled our pews, uncounted statistics of an invisible plague ravaging the Church we all served. This was no innocent, benign policy we espoused toward gays and lesbians; it was actually killing people!

But the real shock came when I realized that the bullet that passed through Jim and struck John had come to rest at my own closet door. In fact, it blew the hinges off that door, making any effort to go on hiding inside totally impossible. Dead and gone was the belief that I could abdicate my authority to preach the gospel and slip away quietly. Rather than hide, I felt compelled by the Holy Spirit to maintain my ordination credentials and come out publicly—regardless of the consequences. Just as God had dealt with me, God wanted me to deal with the Church we both loved on its uncharitable position concerning same-gender orientation.

Surrendering to that call was anything but easy, particularly in light of its impact on the family I loved. I felt far more akin to Jonah resisting the trip to Nineveh than I did an excited Isaiah shouting, "Here I am Lord! Send me!"

But one more time, God won the battle for my heart. In the final months of 1990, I methodically went about the process of *publicly* disclosing my same-gender orientation. As treacherous as the journey felt, the course always remained clear. The Spirit of God spoke up from the depth of my soul, reminding me constantly that disclosure was about integrity, about removing the invisible walls of secrecy and deceit which separated me emotionally from the people I loved. Though I often wanted to turn back, I never really doubted that God had led this moment in time to become what it was. In a sense, that made going on easy, for the suffering and pain of disclosure had purpose: it was the rite of passage into the peace of authenticity—with its gifts of spiritual, emotional, and physical well being.

Before bringing this chapter to a close, I want you to know how remarkable the decade since disclosure has proved to be. Mary and I eventually divorced, and she and the children have done well. Gradually the pounds melted away as authenticity returned my body to good health, and with the surrender to God's will came opportunity for ministry far beyond anything I could ever have imagined.

I moved my counseling practice to Kansas City and now work exclusively with gay married men, their wives, and families—a specialization which others have jokingly said, "puts me in a group of one, nationally." Whatever the case may be, that work has led to the publication of *Just Tell the Truth: Questions*

Families Ask When Gay Married Men Come Out,[1] and to the cofounding of the Norman Institute,[2] a nonprofit educational corporation dedicated to the discovery and dissemination of factual information concerning gender orientation.

And finally, authenticity brought the remarkable opportunity to write this chapter itself. It has given me a chance to help you grasp something of what it's like for gay married clergy to be trapped in a heterosexist church. *But above all else,* it has provided an opportunity to set forth my conviction that the journey toward orientational authenticity is inevitably a spiritual pathway, one along which the traveler finds himself or herself constantly accompanied by a God who simply refuses to go away.

What about the future? Well, I believe the same God that led Terry Norman to authenticity is leading United Methodism today. I believe in the inherent goodness of our denomination and deeply value our long history of social justice. Time and again we have corrected course and made apology for our narrow-minded bigotries of the past. I believe history will prove this to be no less true on the issue of same-gender orientation. The time will come when our Church will apologize to its gay and lesbian members and to the citizens of our country, just as it eventually apologized for its position of slavery in the nineteenth century.

It's only a matter of time until we look back in shame and horror at the soul murder we committed in the name of God. We will lament the fact that we stood by quietly and allowed the so-called religious right to dominate the playing field, allowing others to assume that our silence meant we agreed with their theologically uninformed interpretation of scripture.

I challenge you as United Methodists to use the Wesleyan quadrilateral of scripture, tradition, reason, and experience, and to examine the issue of same-gender orientation for yourself. If God brings you to side with the loyal opposition, then I challenge you to stand with us boldly. Let us proclaim the truth together: namely, that God loves us all just as we are—gay, straight, or in between—and values unconditionally the diversity of gender orientation within the human family.

Notes

1. Terry L. Norman, *Just Tell the Truth: Questions Families Ask When Gay Married Men Come Out* (Kansas City, Mo.: Prehension Publications, 1988).

2. You may visit The Norman Institute on-line at www.NormanInstitute.org, or contact its executive director, Mr. Eddie Miller, by calling (816) 960-7200.

RESISTANCE AND
ECCLESIAL DISOBEDIENCE

Chapter 11 Ignacio Castuera

Dedicated, Disciplined Dissenters

Ecclesiastical Disobedience
and Doctrinal Faithfulness

I did not meet the deadline for this essay due to a series of family crises. This turned out to be providential because now I can write with greater passion and conviction given the fact that Matthew Shepard, a young, brilliant, compassionate, multilingual gay man, was brutally beaten and killed in Wyoming. At his funeral fundamentalist demonstrators from Topeka, Kansas, held placards that read, "Matthew Shepard is burning in hell." At a prayer vigil and press conference in Los Angeles one of the speakers mentioned the website www.godhatesfags.com where one can find pictures of children holding signs with messages echoing the name of the website.

Innumerable editorials appeared across the nation pointing out the correlation between negative epithets and hateful deeds. The murderers of young Matthew Shepard did not operate in a vacuum; rather, they swam in an ocean of prejudice. Their hate crime is only one of the many logical consequences of having ideological (disguised as theological) weapons used long before any objects are employed to bludgeon or shoot those already condemned by words. Jesus was nurtured by a faith that clearly understood the relationship between words and deeds. God's *dabar*, word, was God's deed, and humans, created in God's image, were urged to make their words and deeds coincide.

Christ is for Christians God's Word and Deed made flesh, and his teaching about the correlation of word and deed emerges from this Hebrew matrix of meaning. The teaching in the Gospel of Matthew that one who calls another "racca" is guilty of murder also echoes the correlation of word and deed. It does not matter what this obscure word "racca" means; the point is the logical consequence of using hateful words as a prelude to hateful deeds.

Postponing this essay also makes possible its writing shortly after the courageous and loving act of ninety-seven pastors under the leadership of the Reverend Don Fado, blessing the union of two lesbian members of St. Mark's United Methodist Church in Sacramento. This writing is a poor and feeble attempt to be in solidarity with them and to support their challenge to United Methodist legalists. These legalistic brothers and sisters of ours are only the most recent incarnation of the legalism that is found in Scripture and in the history of the church. They would have us trade our right of primogeniture found in sound theology and doctrine for the lukewarm dish of legislative imperialism. Forgetting that we are the descendants of the one who freed us from the power of the law, our legalistic opponents have joined the previously defunct circumcision party, so deftly defeated by Paul in his letter to the Galatians. By resurrecting this "Tyrannosaurus *Lex*" the neo-Pharisees have joined the ideologues whose words of hate led to the deeds of hate, of which the murder of Matthew Shepard is only the latest, dastardly example.

In light of this situation it is imperative that voices of faithfulness be raised and that the biblical and doctrinal record be revisited to find ways of opposing, in faithfulness to God, the recent incarnation of incantations. One of the time-honored traditions of resistance is disobedience—ecclesiastical and civil disobedience. In our century Gandhi, Rosa Parks, Martin Luther King Jr., Lech Walesa, and many more practiced civil disobedience. Such disobedience is intimately connected to religious convictions and grounded in the biblical teaching that "we must obey God rather than any human authority" (Acts 5:29).

One can summarize the history of our faith without much hyperbole by stating that it is a series of struggles between those who would compartmentalize and codify human behavior in order to please God and those who would depict God as the source of all goodness enabling people to act justly as a response of gratitude to the loving and caring God.

In ancient Israel this division was characterized by the struggles between the priestly class and the prophetic voices. One side insisted on sacrifices, offerings, and rituals to please a God angered by human sin. The other countered that God required mercy, kindness, and justice toward the marginalized, especially that holy trinity of Hebrew Scripture—the widow, the orphan, and the stranger—loosely translated as the sojourner or foreigner.

The destruction of the first temple and the rebuilding of the second make this dispute more acute with Ezra and Nehemiah representing the most extreme, xenophobic form of legalism. Both of these postexilic leaders believed that the racial and religious purity of the people of Israel was the only avenue to ensure God's favor and to prevent further persecution and destruction. It is against this faction that the books of Ruth, Jonah, and Deutero-Isaiah were crafted, all depicting a merciful God whose influence and love extends over all the world and who wishes to move the people from tribal loyalties to world influence. Israel is to be a light to the world not through racial purity and religious punctiliousness but by following God into the new international arena opening before them.

"At the appointed time" Jesus entered history and his followers believed that he sided with the prophetic tradition of Israel over and against the priestly class and the legalists represented by the Pharisees. The early followers of Jesus, however, were unable to avoid the trap that had snared their religious ancestors. Paul, brought up as a Pharisee, saw the light of God's universal love, abandoned the legalism of his upbringing, and opened the doors of the new movement to the Gentiles. From the record we have of Paul's letters and the latter glossings of Luke in the book of Acts, this ministry to the Gentiles was first opposed and then later accepted by some of the early church only on the basis that the Gentiles accept the whole weight of the law, including circumcision. The circumcision party—

apparently led by James and John and supported, at times, by Peter—sent missionaries behind Paul to "correct" his teachings. Paul, a great dissenter, and who was against this group, stated as much in the letter to the Galatians. It is important to note that when the final agreement was hammered out, the "pillars" of the Jerusalem church accepted Paul's ministry to the uncircumcised with the only requirement, gladly accepted by Paul, that the ministry to the poor not be forgotten.

When the Gospels were written, after the destruction of the second temple, the struggles between Jesus and the Pharisees, must be also read as struggles within the budding Jesus movement between those with its universalizing message and the legalistic faction with its new hybrid form in the circumcision party. The Gospel of Mark shows a Pauline influence with a definite anti-Petrine slant. The Gospel of Matthew was influenced by Peter and the circumcision party so much so that Jesus was presented as a New Moses going up to the Mount (the new Sinai) to teach the new law. Yet Matthew began to extend the light of the Gospel toward the Gentiles. Luke is somewhat of a compromise between Mark and Matthew, his genealogy of Jesus goes all the way back to Adam showing the universalizing influences of the Pauline branch of the movement. The Gospel of John modifies the new Moses Christology of Luke by having Jesus issue new teaching not from the mountain but with only one commandment, "that you love one another as I have loved you."

The second and third century of the Common Era found the church in turmoil caught between those who persecuted it from outside and those who sought to split it asunder from inside. Christological controversies abounded and the law and love controversy took either a secondary place or was thinly present in those primary controversies. The triumph of Constantine and his growing acceptance of Christianity—which some still believe was the nadir, not the zenith of Christian history—culminated in the promulgation of the church as the official religion of the Roman Empire.

Part of the reason some people regard the Constantinian intrusion into the life of the church as a mixed blessing at best, has to do with the fact that a newer, "industrial strength"

Christian legalism occurred when the power of the empire was added to the authority of church teaching. Constantine had enough troubles in the secular world and looked to Christianity to provide the unifying glue for the crumbling Roman Empire. When he realized that Christians were also divided, he forced a unity of sorts around an imposed Creed. Christian orthodoxy was thus born more to meet Imperial necessity than to spread divine concern.

By Augustine's day, the church was settled in terms of power but unsettled in terms of doctrine. The main heresies, which Augustine confronted, contained some variation of legalism. Even though my heart goes out to the Donatists—because of the heroism of their martyred bishops—their insistence on certain credentials and personal attributes for celebrants of the sacraments was certainly a form of legalism. Augustine's argument that the efficacy of the Sacrament came from the Sacrament itself and not from the worthiness of its presider was in fact an anti-legalism formula. Augustine was in direct line with the tradition of the church that opposed legalism, and his statement "Love and do as you please" clearly reflected antilegalism sympathies.

The great line of Dedicated, Disciplined Dissenters is difficult to trace between the fifth and sixteenth centuries of our era primarily because many of those dissenters were martyred as heretics. Because of my Hispanic heritage I am mindful of the case of Priscillian of Avila who established a group which included monastic and nonmonastic members. He attracted many women for whom chastity was a definite step up from the exploitation of the kind of marriages prevalent in the Iberian Peninsula and much of the Roman Empire at the time. The rule of law finally won out, and this under the vindictive leadership of bishops whose own character was very questionable. The whole Priscillianist movement was destroyed and much of its leadership massacred. So much for the triumph of law.

The growth and threat of hegemonic Islam aided and abetted the forces of legalism. There was no room for internal dissent in light of the external threat of Islam. The medieval world was a world where the rule of law, church law and secular law, was unquestioned. This also led to a degeneration and disintegration of religious and secular life. There is only time and space here to acknowledge that the paint being used is wide indeed and that some nuances are indeed needed, nevertheless, the world shaped by law ended in little less than lawlessness. Even if one acknowledges a Protestant bias in this judgment, it is indeed true that the world seemed ripe for the Protestant Reformation, a form of dissent, and a reintroduction of the emphases on Grace and Love. From the Council of Constance in 1414 to the sale of indulgences, the Holy Roman Catholic and Apostolic Church was anything but that. Luther's rebellion was ecclesiastical disobedience at its best in light of the unjust "law" under which the church lived at the time. Unlike Wycliffe and Huss who preceded him in rebelling only to end up martyred, Luther succeeded partly because of political and economic realities that did not benefit his worthy predecessors. After his success others followed quickly, Calvin and Zwingli in Switzerland, and all of England under their lusty and lustful King Henry VIII. Alas! In every instance in a matter of a few years legalism reared its head again, and we had Luther threatening the Anabaptists, Calvin refusing to tolerate dissent, and in England violent intolerance, both Protestant and Catholic.

By the time the Americas provided a shelter and haven for those who experienced religious persecution, many would have died in France, England, Ireland, Scotland, and Germany. Intolerance and legalism rained terror over the European scene. What happened to the Roman Catholic Church under the external threat of Islam now was being repeated in the various forms of Protestantism, which was beleaguered from the outside and developed zero tolerance inside. Legalism, once again, was aided and abetted by historical circumstance.

Two hundred years later in England, John Wesley, a priest in the Church of England, also participated in a form of ecclesiastical disobedience that has long been misunderstood. When a fellow priest complained about the violation by John Wesley of church and royal rules that constrained a priest to the borders of a parish, Wesley defiantly replied that he looked upon the whole world as his parish. This ecclesial disobedience of Wesley has unfortunately been passed on as a program for taking the gospel to the whole world. We have now a domesticated and tidied Wesley instead of the adamant street preacher who refused to be bound by what in essence was an unjust law that would not permit him to preach the gospel to those who had been neglected by their own parish priests.

A few years later the followers of Wesley in the new continent would refuse to obey their founder as he appealed for loyalty to King George when the colonies rebelled against unjust taxation. Most followers of Wesley refused to obey their aged leader and instead a new church was born in the midst of rebellion. Unwilling to follow unjust rules the Methodists became part of the group that forged a new nation dedicated to the proposition that all people are created equal. This was seditious teaching from the British perspective but it was the right and righteous thing to do.

The early years of the nineteenth century found Christians in America reliving the grace and law split now around the issue of slavery. Christians in the Northern states could not be bound by the narrow reading of texts which their Southern Christian brothers and sisters claimed to be authoritative proof that slavery was permitted, nay, encouraged by God. By 1848 the Methodist garment could not hold together and two churches were created, one with a narrow, legalistic reading of Scripture that served the institution of slavery, the other open to the prompting of the Spirit and opposed to such literalistic readings of Scripture. In a few years the war of words turned into the bloodiest war this nation has ever known.

The shooting ceased in 1865 but the cold cultural and religious Civil War continues even to our day. The Civil War succeeded in ending slavery but segregation continued for another hundred years. The legalistic readings of the Bible continued to give as much comfort to the segregationists as they had given to their slaveholding ancestors. I do not mean to say that the whole South read the Bible in a legalistic, literalistic way. I had several great professors from the South during my seminary years, and it was they, in fact, who first alerted me to the fact that the Civil War had not exactly ended in 1865 and that modern pastors and politicians were keeping the cinders of legalism hot waiting for the right moment to rekindle them.

Our century has witnessed disobedience primarily in its outer "civil" guise, but from Gandhi to Walesa one can find the religious foundations of their protest. Now given the reality outlined earlier of the resurrection of "the circumcision party," religious disobedience has become imperative. In 1996, fifteen Bishops spoke just before the fateful vote legislating against ministering to those involved in loving, faithful committed relationships with people of the same sex. In 1997 during the season of Epiphany, fifteen pastors sought to bring the light of God's love into the world by supporting the fifteen Bishops and urging the Church to reject the legalism of the winning party in the 1996 General Conference. By 1998 Jimmy Creech in Nebraska and Greg Dell in Illinois had performed "holy unions" in their churches in clear defiance of the legalistic position of our denomination. Some months after the ceremony in Illinois, fifteen hundred people formed a circle of love around the church to counter-protest a gathering staged by the same group from Kansas who had so hatefully demonstrated outside the church at Matthew Shepard's funeral. At the time of this writing, the growing opposition to the unjust law of the Church on homosexuality was crystallized in the Sacramento event where ninety-seven pastors pronounced the blessing over the vows of love, loyalty, and commitment of two sexagenarian women.

This wave of dissent will turn into a tide of creative disobedience. Blind obedience, or as Dorothee Soelle calls it "mere obedience," is contrary to the way of Christ:

> The psychic base for the newer virtues then is no longer obedience that is measured according to norms, which accepts the difficulties of a situation, which supports order and willingly endures that which must be endured. The new base is (Christ's) *phantasie*. In fact it may be said that *phantasie* is the mother of all of tomorrow's virtues—since obedience no longer claims the authority of a father figure, *phantasie* and all of its children are once more free to establish a better kingdom. . . . The *phantasie* of Christ is a *phantasie* of hope, which never gives up anything or anyone and allows concrete reversals to provoke nothing but new discoveries.[1]

What now? I believe that by the time this book is published there will be many more acts of defiant and hopeful *phantasie* and many more gay and lesbian unions or marriages performed by disobedient, yet doctrinally faithful, United Methodists. Will this mean that United Methodist conferences will be mired in interminable Church trials similar to the one the nation is experiencing right now in the halls of Congress? Will all of us learn that legalism is not the answer to the issue before us? Will models of dialogue emerge to avoid the self-destructive path of Church trials? I write this essay in the sincere hope that these essays and the courageous acts of my clergy brothers and sisters will constitute a clarion call to dialogue. The issue of homosexuality in the Church defies legislation. We must learn to live together in constant prayer and dialogue. We must apply to ourselves the same wisdom that the people who agreed on the books to be included in the canon of the Bible applied for their time. Our ancestors in the faith did not opt for either/or solutions. The xenophobic books of Ezra and Nehemiah were not thrown out; our parents in the faith simply added the dissenting positions of Ruth, Jonah, and Deutero-Isaiah. Instead of settling for one Gospel the church leaders opted to include four with very different christologies. The imminent eschatology of Paul was not excised; instead the Petrine epistles were allowed in to help explain the delay of the Parousia. God is once more calling us to learn to live together, to struggle together, to learn together. Out of the chiaro-scuro of our opposing positions God will weave a new and exciting pattern for the Church in the twenty-first century. Blind obedience will only lead us into the darkness of single issues and simpleminded solutions. Let us stay together as contrasting positions that might just become complementary in a future that only God can see.

Notes

1. This is my own translation. I have left the German word *phantasie* alone because it is much richer than the English word *fantasy*. See Dorothee Soelle's *Beyond Mere Obedience: Reflections on a Christian Ethic for the Future*, trans. Lawrence W. Denef (Minneapolis: Augsburg Publishing House, 1970), pp. 76-78.

Chapter 12 *Joretta L. Marshall*

Ecclesial Disobedience as a Spiritual Discipline

The church is a place where conflict over competing concerns is as present as elsewhere in the world. It is a community that structures itself in ways that encourage some normative and agreed upon understandings or rules by which we might live together. At the same time, faithful Christians have known throughout history that rules, by themselves, cannot contain the creative and redemptive power of God. In fact, at times, persons have been called to disobey one set of rules in order to seek justice at deeper levels. The faith is made whole in persons who continue to believe that rules and legal systems—even those of the church—sometimes must be challenged, and perhaps, disobeyed. Initially, we do not know the cost of such prophetic witness, just as we do not know the rewards that might eventuate from these endeavors. We participate faithfully in disobedience in the belief that the best discernment occurs in communities where multiple voices are heard and honored, even when there might be deep disagreement about the validity of the claims of some of the participants.

The presence of women and men who challenge church structures as part of their commitment to the gospel is diverse. A growing number of clergy and laity wonder aloud about the "rules" as they are applied to those who can and cannot be ordained, who can and cannot be married, and who can and cannot participate in ritual moments for lesbians and gays. Members of the church universal struggle with questions of obedience to polity, not out of mere political strategizing, but out of a genuine commitment to live faithfully. Clergy who are prohibited from serving members of their congregations who are lesbian and gay, or even from serving any congregation until they agree to end their disobedience, find it more and more difficult to remain within the structure of the church. Laity, either because of their sexual orientation or because of their commitment to justice, experience the church as oppressive and struggle with decisions about leaving the institution. We find ourselves in a maze of fear, suspicion, conflict, and tension as we attempt to mediate the various moral claims pronounced in the name of society, God, and the church.

Many laity and clergy—straight, lesbian, gay, bisexual—are convinced that the current rules of the institutional church do not fulfill the best vision for God's community, particularly as they apply to persons in same-gender relationships or to those who serve them as pastors and friends. More clergy are vocal and public in their disobedience as they respond to the gospel in the context of the congregations and communities that they serve. The fear of counteractions of restraint and reprimand from the institutional church is more than an empty threat. The risk for each one who participates in some form of disobedience is as varied as the manner in which we quietly or publicly disobey the polity of our respective denominations. It is to these persons that many of us owe gratitude and thanks, for their communal practice of ecclesial disobedience—consciously disobeying church polity because of moral convictions—embodies the redemptive ministry of the institutional church.

This article does not argue the moral complexities of homosexuality since there are numerous resources that provide substantive discussions on these issues. My perspective affirms and sanctifies lesbians, gays, bisexuals, and their intimate sexual relationships when these relationships embody the normative values of love, justice, and mutual concern. In addition, I hold the perspective that lesbians, gays, and bisexuals can make exemplary models of faithful spiritual leaders among the ordained and laypeople of the church.

In this essay I want to address two closely related issues. First, I want to name the reality of the heterosexism that lives within the culture and that invades the church. Understanding heterosexism as an inherent form of systemic, political, legal, and moral injustice points to the need to address the issues not only from the standpoint of political action, but from a religious, theological, and spiritual perspective. Heterosexism in the church raises our consciousness about the need for ecclesial disobedience in the very institution in which we live. Second, and more important, I want to suggest that spiritual leaders— lay and ordained—who are engaged in liberating the church from the heterosexist ties that bind us, and who practice some form of ecclesial disobedience, would be well served to understand their actions as part of their spiritual discipline. Until such a time as the church changes, more and more of us will be called to participate in active and public ecclesial disobedience. We can do this either out of a movement of social protest and resistance alone, or we can do this out of a genuine understanding of the spiritual life and leadership to which we are called. While the former is needed for every liberation movement, there are many of us for whom ecclesial disobedience is not only a public statement, but a spiritual discipline that points to the depth of our living relationship with God.

Heterosexism and the Church

Heterosexism is defined as those structures that shape and mold persons at societal, communal, interpersonal, and internal levels to embrace and embody a heterosexual orientation and way of being in the world. Heterosexuals are encouraged to live their lives and are protected by laws that attempt to guarantee rights, jobs, families, and financial status. For example, no one can be fired from a job for talking about an opposite-sex partner or date, as long as that is done within the confines of appropriate discourse. In addition, unless one is neglectful or abusive, no one can take children from heterosexual partners who remain married to each other. Likewise, family members who are related by legal marriage, blood, or adoption may be added to one's insurance plan without many complications or questions. If a heterosexual spouse is in the emergency room, the opposite-sex spouse is usually considered to be the next of kin.

However, as we know, these same statements cannot be made about those who self-identify as bisexual, lesbian, or gay. While the church often battles for civil rights in the context of the culture, there is great irony in the probability that someone will lose a job in the church because of his or her sexual orientation. Rarely does the institutional church encourage or sanctify committed partnerships between same-sex adults or the honest parenting of children in ways that affirm lesbians, gays, and bisexuals as faithful persons. It is impossible in most mainline denominations for persons of same-sex orientation openly to secure employment. Heterosexism is perpetrated in the name of the church in ways to which religious people would protest if these actions were part of other institutions in our culture. A seemingly contradictory set of claims is made by the church: it is all right for those who self-identify as lesbians/gays/bisexuals to worship (if they find a church in which they feel comfortable), but they are not capable of leading worship as ordained persons unless, of course, they dance around definitions of statements such as "celibacy in singleness and fidelity in marriage." The church's silence, and at times its vociferous reaction against lesbians, gays, and bisexuals, have encouraged many of us to break from the structures of churches we joined initially with the intention to sustain our spirits. In an institution that seeks to advocate for basic freedoms for all people, heterosexism is pervasive in church life as we neglect to protect individuals and couples whose love is best expressed through the intimacy of same-sex partnerships.

In response to the heterosexism to which we bear witness, many of us who live within the boundaries of the church have participated in the past and continue to participate in some form of ecclesial disobedience. Some of us are ordained, spending the rest of our careers watching for those who would take away that privilege of service. Others are laypersons who are the invisibly visible, present in the pews of our churches every Sunday, taking active leadership roles, sometimes noticed and welcomed as powerful lay leaders, and at other times rendered invisible by virtue of their sexuality. Others work at the structural levels of the church to change systems or to protect those who are lesbians and gay men from being "outed" to the rest of the church or dismissed from its service. Still others stand on the margins of the lesbian and gay community, knowing that being faithful to the church alienates us from the community of sisters and brothers who have left the church because of the pain of not being welcomed as sacred beings who are worthy of the church's love and respect.

Heterosexism is destroying the soul of the church. It is killing the spirits of lesbians, gay men, bisexuals, family members, friends, and others who are moved to be faithful and who expect the church to embody the grace and power of God's justice. Under such assault, it is imperative that we turn to a spiritual discipline of ecclesial disobedience in whatever form we might be able to risk personally, communally, and as a church.

Ecclesial Disobedience as Spiritual Discipline

The art of spiritual discipline speaks of our relationship with God as it is embodied in our relationships with others and with the world around us. Prayer, meditation, centering activities, and communal worship are ways in which we not only approach God, but also ways in which we seek to respond to the call of God in our lives. Spiritual discipline is required in order that we may know and experience the fullness of God and continue to explore the richness and depths of God's diverse presence in the world.

Ecclesial disobedience can be simply a matter of protest against an injustice, and does not necessarily have to relate to the practice of a spiritual discipline. However, for those who wish to discern if, when, or how to disobey the polity of a denomination on moral, theological, and spiritual grounds, it would be wise to understand the spiritual dimensions of such disobedience. There are three ways in which ecclesial disobedience can be part of a more comprehensive spiritual discipline.

First, spiritual disciplines nurture and clarify our faith. Through our spiritual practices we gain a deeper knowledge of the gospel and its meaning in our lives. We recognize that acts of courage and honesty confront the structures and content of our faith in ways that make us more readily able to hear the call of God in our lives. Ecclesial disobedience, as part of a spiritual discipline, lays claim to the reality that God's illuminating activities cannot be confined in the polity of a denomination.

To participate in such disobedience as a spiritual discipline requires that persons and communities continually confront their assumptions about what God is asking from us and how God is working among us. This suggests spiritual attitudes that carry with them sincere discernment and a faithfulness of intentions, seeking to bring God's justice to the community of faith through prayer and other embodiments of faith. Spiritual practices assist us in gaining insight, clarity, and perception about the multidimensionality of God's truth. We practice such disciplines in the hopes of deepening and nurturing the faith on which we stand. Those of us who participate in ecclesial disobedience as a part of our spiritual discipline do so not because we intend to break the rules, but because we intend to follow the call of the gospel even when it means going against the normative polity of a denomination.

Second, the art of spiritual discipline assists in developing and bearing witness to the humble courage necessary to live out our faith. There is a certain humility that must come with ecclesial disobedience; it is the humility that one might be passionate, but wrong about a particular issue or about one's approach to an issue. Likewise, humility notes that the church might stand in the wrong on the same issue. Together as a community of faith there is an attempt to discern a truth that can live into the gospel message. Spiritual discipline is done with intense passion, but not with arrogance. Acting on one's conscience requires a commitment to ongoing conversation. The discussions must be not only with those with whom one agrees, but also with those whom one believes are wrong in their discernment. It can take incredible courage and humility to remain at the table of conversation.

For many of us who constantly make choices that put our ministries at risk, there is an underlying tenet that our faith is evident in our staying power or our resistance to abandon the church. In other words, for some of us the willingness to stay when it would be easier on our emotional, physical, and even spiritual lives to leave the church embodies a fundamental belief in the importance of resisting dominant structures and remaining open to the voice of God's call in new ways. Many of us stay not because we are martyrs or heroes, but because of our faithful call to stand for something that points toward the good news. Staying in the church with integrity, however, often takes its toll on our spiritual lives. Bitterness and anger not only fuels our righteous indignation, but they also simply wear us out. Only when there is a significant number of persons staying with us, standing with us, and walking with us are we able to stay with some sense of the abundance of life intact. To bear humble witness to the gospel requires a spiritual depth that must be nurtured with care.

Finally, practicing the art of ecclesial disobedience as a spiritual discipline can enhance our sense of communal connection. Participation in disobedience should not be done on a whim, nor should it be practiced out of anger, hatred, or isolation. Instead, ecclesial disobedience must be practiced as a spiritual discipline that enlists the support and thought of a community to which one is held accountable. Such acts of conscience must happen in the context of a community and not be the activity of lone individuals who are out to prove a point. It is too easy to act in isolation and then to feel betrayed when others do not interpret the gospel in the same manner or when we feel abandoned by the community that we think supports us. The purpose of disobedience must be not vengeance; rather, the act of disobedience should be an invitation to change the systems and structures of which we are a part. These systems connect us as a community of faith. Only when we address the structures and inherent injustices as a community will transformation occur at the deepest spiritual levels.

Persons practicing this form of faithfulness ought to take considerable care to protect others and to be accountable ultimately to those communities on whose behalf one is trying to advocate—lesbians and gay men in the instance of heterosexism.

Similarly, such disobedience requires one to be willing to bear
the risk of consequences for one's self, but should not expect
others to participate in the process without careful and prayerful
thought. Such a discipline requires communal courage and honesty of heart, mind, and soul. In sum, it requires a process of discernment as communities, and individuals within communities,
carefully count the potential gains and losses of disobedience.
We need leaders who can afford to practice the art of ecclesial
disobedience on behalf of lesbians and gay men, our families, our
relationships, and our ways of being faithful in the world.

I, like many of my colleagues who teach in mainline denominational or independent schools of theology, grow weary of seeing some of the brightest and most capable of our students turn
from ministry—or be turned from ministry—because they are not
willing to be silent about their sexual orientation or about their
commitments to those who are lesbian or gay. The number of students who approach me, and others like myself, to ask wisdom
about filling out ordination papers and meeting with boards of
ministries, presbyteries, diocesan committees, and other denominational groups are more than many of us can count. The spring
of the year is particularly full of pain, anger, and anguish as persons spend inordinate amounts of energy to adjudicate between
their call to ministry and their call to be true to their understanding of God's created goodness by living out of their bisexual, lesbian, or gay orientations with integrity. There are also a number
of students who struggle with whether they can commit to a
church that they experience as being heterosexist and abusive in
its structure. We continue to lose potentially faithful and gifted
spiritual leaders because of our reluctance to be transformed.

Many closeted clergy are dependent upon the good graces of
others in the system to "protect" them. Those who choose the
route of ordination end up spending a lot of energy being careful lest they step outside the bounds and say something they
shouldn't or disclose to someone who will turn them in to others in the denomination. This constant anxiety and concern
result in a loss of attention to the other demands and needs of
the church on the part of everyone. It is difficult to be free in
one's care and outpouring when one's energy is being consumed

with the task of discernment about with whom one can be safe, whom one needs to fear, and how to walk careful lines lest someone be "caught." The life-giving energy that calls persons into ministry is lost in the overwhelming reality of constant decision making about how to survive the systems of ministry.

There is an incredible sadness as those churches where students once found refuge and sanctuary for their souls have now become places where students' gifts and graces are not only unwelcome, but where it is unsafe to be who they feel called to be. Experiences of a church that struggles to live into the gospel are replaced with experiences of a church that lives in fear and trembling of conflict and debate. The gifts of the church are lost to individuals; the gifts of individuals are lost to the collective community. This is not the way I imagine God calling the church to embody the presence of a Living and Dynamic Spirit.

Ecclesial disobedience is a spiritual practice for faithful persons who, vocally or quietly, assume that the rules of the church need to change. These persons are willing to protect those whose lives hang in the balance by speaking when others are silent or silenced. Their prophetic witness is evident as they carefully advise lesbians or gay men who approach them seeking clarity about ordination. They promote respect and care without demanding a sharing of knowledge that jeopardizes one's vocational call. As a part of their spiritual leadership in the church, they participate in life-giving rituals for lesbians and gay men that support and enhance their relationships, even when the church and the state refuse to offer them the ecclesial and legal apparatus for doing so. Those who practice ecclesial disobedience do so with conviction, clarity, and humility.

Conclusion

What is at stake in our deliberations about heterosexism are not simply the rights of those of us who self-identify as lesbian, gay, or bisexual. What is at stake are the lives and souls of the churches of which we are a part. What is at stake are the lives and souls of the very same churches in which many of us were nurtured and loved. Our communities of faith stand the greatest to lose—and hence, the greatest to gain—in this struggle. I have little doubt that, eventually, the legal system will make progress in the arena of civil rights for lesbians and gays. I am less hopeful, at times, that the liberative aspects of the church will lead the way or that some of us will stay alive spiritually through the journey. Yet, the movement of the Spirit continues even as those of us in religious establishments, in denominational structures, and in places of academia learn to trust our voices once again and use them collectively in careful and prophetic ways. My deepest hope is that there are enough who have the power and ability to practice the spiritual discipline of ecclesial disobedience so that the church's transformation will be led by a creative and redemptive Spirit.

Those of us who have something to gain in this process—those of us who are seeking a faithful response to heterosexism—need to find ways to honor and support those who would dare to act in ecclesial disobedience. It is with passion and compassion that some of us must practice the spiritual discipline of ecclesial disobedience. Our passion must be rooted in our search for a church of God that embodies justice for all, creating a new vision for the world around us. It must also be done with the knowledge that none of us knows the complete truth, but together we might live faithfully in a world that requires justice.

Yet, we must also approach our task with compassion for one another, for those who have as yet to understand how much we are losing by our refusal to be bearers of the good news, and for those with whom we disagree. We need to practice compassionate support for those clergy who welcome and promote healthy living for lesbians and gays, who offer rituals of transition and celebrations of commitments, or who live as closeted lesbians and gays. We cannot leave the task of liberation from heterosexism in the church up to the lesbians, bisexuals, and gay men who remain among our numbers. Instead, it is up to the church—all of us—to practice the spiritual discipline of ecclesial disobedience. The church has everything to lose and everything to gain. Let us give thanks for those who understand ecclesial disobedience as part of their passionate and compassionate call on behalf of the church.

Chapter 13   *J. Philip Wogaman*

Conscience and Ecclesial Disobedience

I have not always been opposed to the stance of The United Methodist Church on homosexuality. I do not recall paying much attention to the specific language on the subject when the Social Principles were adopted in 1972, but I would have agreed then that the practice of homosexuality is incompatible with Christian teaching. I am not a biblical fundamentalist, so my positions on such issues have never been based on a few isolated verses of scripture used as proof texts.

Nevertheless, homosexuality just seemed contrary to nature, contrary to the way God has created us. Moreover, I was a bit offended by what I took to be intellectual overreaching and manipulation by advocates in the gay community. Even so, I felt that issues related to homosexuality were not all that important. As a Christian ethicist, teaching on a theological faculty, I was concerned about issues I considered much more important.[1] If homosexual practice is a sin, I thought, surely it is not a major one.

A Change of Understanding

My views have changed gradually. Greater contact with gay and lesbian persons in the 1970s at least made me more tolerant. By 1984 I opposed the General Conference action of that year prohibiting ordination of self-avowed practicing homosexuals. I considered it wrong to single this out, and I believed annual conferences perfectly capable of judging candidates for ministry without that kind of direction from the general church. Elected to the General Conference for the first time in 1988, I was struck by the inflamed rhetoric of letters and resolutions I received before the Conference convened. I was among those who worked for the establishment of what came to be called the Committee to Study Homosexuality. I hoped that process could help the church to understand why some people are homosexual and others are not and, at the same time, clarify the theological issues.

As a member of the committee, I was disappointed that we were not able to gain closure on the biological issues. No scientific theory of the nature of homosexuality—or heterosexuality, for that matter—has yet gained broad acceptance among eminent investigators in the field. It may in fact prove to be the case that homosexuality and heterosexuality are caused by a complex interconnection between physiological, psychological, and sociological factors.

As to the capacity of gay and lesbian persons changing their orientation, it is clear that many homosexuals, having accepted their orientation as a blessing from God, feel no calling to change. Moreover, the committee's scientific consultants were not at all in agreement on whether it is even possible for gay and lesbian persons to change their orientation any more than it is for heterosexuals to do so. My own impression, gained partly from study and partly from individuals I have known, is that some who seek to change their patterns of behavior (and possibly even their orientation) do so while most do not find it possible even when they so wish. It is arbitrary and cruel to tell those who want to change and are not able to do so that they can if they just try harder or if they will surrender more to Christ.

What has had the largest impact on my own thinking has been more contact with gay and lesbian persons and their loved ones. We interviewed many in the course of the committee's study, and in my ministry at Foundry Church since 1992 I have gotten to know many more. These are real people, not abstractions. Many are people of Christian commitment, moral integrity, and authentic spirituality. In the broader gay community and among heterosexuals there are doubtless those who fit the description of moral decadence to be found in the first chapter of Paul's Letter to the Romans.[2] But it now seems very clear to me that there are also many gay and lesbian Christians who are not like that at all. I still do not know why they are gay or lesbian and not heterosexual like me, but I cannot any longer consider them to be less normal or Christian than I am or than their critics are. Sweeping condemnations of all gay and lesbian persons hurt really good people, both by reinforcing a social stigma with which they must contend and by attacking their own sense of self-worth. The standard formula "love the sinner and hate the sin" conveys an ominous message to people whose sexual orientation is defined as a greater disposition toward sin. Burdens of guilt and social disapproval are inflicted needlessly upon many gay and lesbian people. It is a terrible wrong.

Assessing the Church's Message

How much change is needed in the message of The United Methodist Church? Some of that message is really very good. The sections of the Social Principles dealing with sexuality are not all that bad taken as a whole. For instance, we acknowledge sexuality as a good gift of God—which surely it is, not only for purposes of procreation but as an expression of love. We are conscious that it is a gift that can be misused—which surely it can be. When sexual expression is disconnected from love and commitment, one's spiritual integrity is undermined. When sexuality is used exploitatively, persons are injured, sometimes for a lifetime. The Social Principles point to such things with clarity. Certainly all of the things said about sexual exploitation apply as much to homosexuality as to heterosexuality. One can also appreciate the language of grace—noting that all of us, whether homosexual or heterosexual, stand in need of God's grace, and that the church's ministry must be an expression of that grace. Moreover, there is a fine paragraph on human rights for homosexual persons, insisting that laws protect homosexual persons from abuse while also protecting such persons in their relationships.

But there are other parts of the Church's message that have become increasingly heavy-handed. Gays and lesbians are singled out to be ineligible—as a class—for ordination. The practice of homosexuality is identified as incompatible with Christian teaching. Clergy are not to conduct ceremonies that celebrate homosexual unions nor are such ceremonies to be held in United Methodist churches. Church funds are not to be used to advance the acceptance of homosexuality—a prohibition some interpret as prohibiting ordinary educational materials about homosexuality except those labeling it as sinful. It seems that each General Conference must add to the list. There is an element of hysteria in all this. Why has this subject gotten so inflamed? Why does it matter so much?

I find it revealing that the Social Principles cannot say how or why the practice of homosexuality is (necessarily and always) contrary to Christian teaching. The General Conference debates on the subject do not help much. Reasons given have ranged from a kind of selective biblical literalism (a biblical literalism applied only to this subject) to natural law arguments. Most of the arguments have been pretty superficial. More to the point, nothing could be placed in the Social Principles that would constitute persuasive teaching because the Church as such simply does not have a coherent position on the subject. The best it can do is to announce conclusions based primarily on inherited views and prejudices.

Perhaps this would not matter overmuch, were it not that real people are being hurt by this part of the Church's message. It is, of course, argued that the practice of homosexuality itself is what hurts people, and that the Church does well to issue serious warnings. But the Church does not know that homosexuality hurts people. In light of the disagreements and the admitted lack of sufficient knowledge about the nature and causes of homosexuality, the Church would be more faithful if it would be more humble. Why not acknowledge that some of us believe this, and others believe that, and that we do not yet have the basis, as a church, for a real consensus? We could, with grace, treat homosexuality like other issues upon which the Church does not have a common view and leave the question open as a humble acknowledgment of our differences.

Acting Within the Church's Covenant

There remains the question, How should people act in faithfulness when they find the Church's teaching and practice in conflict with their Christian conscience? It is one thing to say that we should all work to change the teaching and practices with which we are in disagreement. I take it that is always in order, although I note that some who support the present condemnations of homosexuality are offended that those of us who disagree with them keep bringing the subject up. Of course we do! That is why we keep having General Conferences. God always has more for us to chew on. What would have happened to our Church, morally speaking, if we had concluded back in the 1950s that we should give up trying to change the Church's structures of racial segregation because several General Conferences in a row had been unwilling to change them? Serious efforts to change Church teaching on homosexuality can be predicted until there is a deeper consensus about what the teachings ought to be—or until the Church is willing to acknowledge the presence of principled differences among people of good faith. So efforts to bring change continue to be in order.

What about obedience to Church law and teaching as they currently exist, even as we seek change? A powerful case can be made that as a part of a covenanting community of faith, we have such an obligation. Practically speaking, we all have a stake in faithfulness to the covenant since our ability to expect obedience from our adversaries when we prevail is contingent upon our obedience when they prevail even as we all continue to work for change. That principle of covenant has ancient roots in secular philosophy as well as persuasive theological grounding. Practically speaking, the principle is an "article of peace"—a necessary condition of maintaining a harmonious community in spite of conflict and disagreement. Theologically speaking, the principle is both a recognition that any of us may be wrong and that even when we are not wrong we are constrained to love our adversaries and to respect them. God is greater than any of us. When we disagree with a position taken by the Church, we should reflect that God may be speaking through that majority. Respect for the covenant should therefore be given great weight.

In light of this, I am not surprised that some in The United Methodist Church were critical of the actions of the Reverend Jimmy Creech and of the jury that acquitted him of the charge of violating Church law. Why, then, did I myself testify in his behalf at that trial? My testimony centered largely around the question of whether there was a sufficient basis in church law for treating his actions at the ceremony of commitment between two lesbians as a chargeable offense. I did not believe he had actually violated the covenant. Even if he had, I believe he acted in conscience in an area loaded with ambiguity, and I felt the Church court needed to find a way to respect and accommodate that.

Ecclesial Disobedience

Of course, the Church covenant, while deserving of great respect, is not God. And our commitment to that covenant, serious as it should be, cannot be an absolute. When there is a conflict between our loyalty to church law and our loyalty to God, clearly God must come first. What are we to say, then, about theologically and morally principled disobedience to Church law?

The first thing I want to say is that the Church should try hard not to place its members and ordained ministers in a position where they are forced to choose between their conscience and their obedience to the covenant—where one's conscience is on collision course with one's community of faith. Such collisions cannot always be avoided, either in secular society or in the church, but the conscience of our members and leaders is one of the Church's most precious assets. People on both sides of conflicts of conscience should do everything possible to honor and accommodate the views of their opponents. It is not always possible. But do we always try as hard as we should?

What are we to do when we find ourselves seriously opposed to church law and no effort was made to accommodate our conscience? A tempting answer is just to leave. Some would say that it is generally the only principled thing to do. But how many truly committed people of the Church want to do that? Most of us will not lightly abandon the community in which our faith and our spiritual life have been nurtured and where we have many valued relationships. We also recognize that important issues can become clearer, and that perceptions change over time. "New occasions teach new duties" and "time makes ancient good uncouth."[3] The Methodist Episcopal Church split over slavery in 1844. By 1939, it was clear to nearly everybody that slavery was wrong. Reunion in 1939 was purchased at the expense of African Americans, who were forced to endure three more decades of official segregation. In 1888, Frances Willard, a woman properly elected as a delegate to General Conference, was refused her proper place. In 1988 that woman's leadership was celebrated at a General Conference session with Bishop Leontine Kelly as presiding officer. Historical perspective on the evolution of these and other conflicts leads me to believe that most often it is better for us all to stay together and work at the resolution of issues.

What can one do, short of leaving? A further possibility is to conform to the absolute letter of the law, while taking advantage of every remaining loophole or possibility that the law has not anticipated—that is, observing the *letter* but not the *spirit* of the law. Is that justifiable? Perhaps it depends on what one perceives the spirit of the law to be. We are not obliged to obey the spirit of a mean-spirited law. In the case of United Methodist teaching and law on the subject of homosexuality, the spirit seems to be quite mixed. In part, it seems to be formed by grace and solicitous of the human rights of oppressed people. In part, it seems bent upon ensuring that the practice of homosexuality will be thoroughly rejected, even stigmatized, in every form and in spite of every evidence of the Holy Spirit in the lives of homosexual persons. What are we to do when the two spirits are in conflict?

Sometimes it is possible to conform to the letter of the law, narrowly interpreted, while acting wherever possible in accordance with a more generous spirit and grace. Is that being faithful to the covenant? Perhaps it is, for laws framed in a legalistic spirit invite minimal legalistic compliance. And it is certainly faithful to the deeper theological meaning of the covenant. What could that mean in respect to a church law prohibiting clergy from officiating in ceremonies of commitment of same-gender couples? Perhaps a pastor, not being authorized as a representative of the Church to define this as a marriage, could nevertheless acknowledge that the couple has already made a commitment to each other and then, in prayer, to ask God's blessing upon them.

In respect to the ordination of self-avowed homosexuals, the Church has at least wisely chosen not to invite official witch-hunts. So legalism might dictate the avoidance of self-avowal by gays and lesbians who feel called to exercise ministry while remaining quiet about their sexual orientation. We can honor those who choose to pay the price of avowing their sexual orientation publicly, but I do not question the integrity of those who choose rather to be quiet and remain in ministry. In any event, it is not ecclesial disobedience so long as one conforms to the letter of the law. I do grieve that the church feels it must confront good people with such choices, particularly because of the church's singular inability to provide a theologically and scientifically convincing rationale.

What are we to say about real ecclesial disobedience? A number of pastors have formally conducted ceremonies of committed union for homosexual persons, clearly in violation of the recent Judicial Council ruling. How are we to evaluate what appears to be an act of defiance?

In the literature on civil disobedience, a standard principle is that one must be willing to face the consequences when one disobeys a law for conscience' sake. There are exceptions to such a principle, as I have noted elsewhere.[4] For instance, the

Underground Railroad to aid escaping slaves in antebellum times depended for its effectiveness on secrecy. In similar fashion, there may be pastors who privately conduct ceremonies of union precisely to avoid negative consequences. But what about those who, in conscience, are prepared to disobey such a church law openly and to take the consequences? That can surely be an expression of good conscience.

The question then shifts to what the consequences should be. Church law (at least in The United Methodist Church) lists a variety of possible penalties, but without specifying which should apply. That is left up to local or regional authorities who must ascertain the facts, evaluate the degree of seriousness, assess the behavior and motives of the one being tried. If the law itself shows little respect for the conscience of one who has felt compelled to disobey it, those charged with enforcement can certainly show greater sensitivity. For example, if pastors are convicted in the current trials over the conducting of unions, it is not necessary that the penalty be loss of ministerial status. It could be that the courts of one's peers might conclude that a simple reprimand is more appropriate. The penalty is determined by those who really know the situation and the people involved. The consequences of principled noncompliance with a rule can at least be mitigated by those who respect the conscience of the person charged with the offense.

Of course, ecclesial disobedience is more justified in some situations than others. We have all known people who were so full of being "right" that they had forgotten how to be good. Christian conscience is not abstract rightness, to be honored at all cost just for its own sake. Sometimes our sense of rightness must yield to a majority within the community of faith who disagree with us—if just being "right" is all that is at stake. There is a deeper level of Christian conscience, however. That is a conscience formed by our response to God's grace in Jesus Christ and engaged in our love of others.

Most of those in the Church who contemplate ecclesial disobedience of rules affecting gay and lesbian people are not so much concerned about being right as they are about protecting and supporting fellow human beings who are being stigmatized.

Gay and lesbian persons of demonstrated competence and high moral character have been excluded from pastoral ministry. Gay and lesbian persons are tortured by the message that they must change in order to become acceptable, despite abundant evidence that they will not be able to change in that way. Perhaps most ironic, gay and lesbian persons are told that promiscuity is sinful, but at the same time also told that the church will not support their committed unions—and that it will punish those who seek to offer such support. Archbishop Desmond Tutu's comments on this are worth repeating here:

> We reject them, treat them as pariahs, and push them outside the confines of our church communities. . . . We make them doubt that they are the children of God, and this must be nearly the ultimate blasphemy. We blame them for something that it is becoming increasingly clear they can do little about. . . . Why should we want all homosexual persons not to give expression to their sexuality in loving acts? Why don't we use the same criteria to judge same-sex relationships that we use to judge whether heterosexual relationships are wholesome or not? . . . The Lord of the church would not be where his church is in this matter.[5]

People like Archbishop Tutu are not as concerned about being "right" as they are about responding with Christlike love to people who are being hurt by church teaching and law. It is one thing to defer to a majority whom we consider to be mistaken on an issue of principle, confident that we will be able to continue the dialogue and perhaps one day to prevail. It is another thing to abandon vulnerable people.

Notes

1. It is surprising, in retrospect, that I had almost nothing to say on the subject in my *Christian Method of Moral Judgment* (London: SCM Press; Philadelphia: Westminster Press, 1976) and that only in 1989 did I begin to address homosexuality in published works.

2. I cite Romans 1 because it is clearly the most serious of the handful of biblical passages dealing with what we now call homosexuality. Actual moral criteria can be drawn from that passage, embodying reasons why homosexual behavior reflects separation from God. But, while the description fits in some cases—doubtless known to Paul, in

other cases it does not. Of course, Paul's list of sins there is wide-ranging enough to include the self-righteousness of many who condemn all homosexual practice.

3. From "Once to Every Man and Nation," *The Book of Hymns* (Nashville: The United Methodist Publishing House, 1966), p. 242.

4. J. Philip Wogaman, *Christian Perspectives on Politics* (Philadelphia: Fortress Press; London: SCM Press, 1988), p. 206.

5. Desmond M. Tutu, foreword to Marilyn Bennett Alexander and James Preston, *We Were Baptized Too: Claiming God's Grace for Lesbians and Gays* (Louisville: Westminster John Knox Press, 1996), pp. ix-x.

RESISTANCE: LEAVING THE CHURCH

Chapter 14   *John Kruse*

Friendly to Liberty?

We support The United Methodist Church with our prayers; but after the August 1998 Judicial Council decision, making pastors who conduct celebrations of homosexual union subject to trial, we have chosen to put our presence, gifts, and service elsewhere. No longer experiencing Methodism as the force for social justice it once was, and because our family includes those who have made holy union covenants, my wife and I no longer feel comfortable being part of a United Methodist congregation.

This decision was emotionally hard because of all that the Methodist Church has meant to us. In college our minds and hearts were shaped by the Methodist Student Movement, *Motive* magazine, and summer work camps. Seminary was a liberating experience as Scripture and Tradition became alive and understandable to me. Serving in campus ministry, we found the Methodist Church on the forefront of the civil rights and anti-war movements. Then, in a succession of congregations, we felt the nourishing presence of supportive communities seeking to minister in the spirit of Christ's love. But we also felt a growing division within the denomination, such that in my retirement statement to the 1994 Wisconsin Annual Conference I wrote:

In spite of Scriptural verses indicating that the earth is flat; I affirm a round, global earth, and cherish that view of this planet which sees it as one home for all of God's children.

The church's resistance to a round earth, citing a half-dozen Bible verses, has been a pattern for resisting the inclusiveness of God's love. Various members of the church have pulled out a favorite few verses to substantiate, at one time or another: the superiority of the white race, the subordination of women, the damnation of those with differing opinions, or the exclusion of homosexual persons from full participation in the church. Scripture obviously needs interpretation. It would seem as if we clergy have been a part of a conspiracy to keep from the laity what we have learned in United Methodist seminaries about the Scriptures and the inclusiveness of God's love.

Yet, since the time of my ordination, I have witnessed the abolition of the Central Jurisdiction, the ordination of women and their election to the episcopacy, the open assertion of the rights of gay and lesbian persons in the church, the breakdown of Catholic/Protestant enmity, and an awareness of other world religions as ethical, human responses to the God beyond gods. I have sensed the spirit of Christ always moving us to greater inclusiveness.

I no longer sense this movement within The United Methodist Church. The 1996 General Conference action which placed a ban on holy unions into the Social Principles, and the Judicial Council decision which interpreted this Principle as law, have, I believe, significantly altered The United Methodist Church in several ways.

1) In the struggle for civil rights for gay and lesbian persons, The United Methodist Church is now officially in the camp of the oppressors.

Africans in America, the 1998 PBS television series which traced America's journey through slavery, documents the attempted slave uprising of 1800 in Richmond, Virginia. We hear the words of one of the conspirators: "All the whites were to be massacred except the Quakers, the Methodists, and the Frenchmen; and they were to be spared on account of their being friendly to liberty." If we could only say that about United Methodists today in the current struggle by homosexual persons to attain civil liberties and a status of dignity, free from harassment and discrimination!

The recent Judicial Council decision, along with the pursuant witch-hunt mentality in the church, indicates to me that our denomination has come down on the side of oppression and persecution. The former ambiguity of the Social Principles, which allowed people of differing opinions to work together, has been replaced by a legal rigidity which subjects to trial those who act according to their conscience in support of gay and lesbian couples. Those in the gay and lesbian community who feel society's hostility are not likely to see United Methodists as "friendly to liberty."

By drawing this parallel between the Abolitionist movement and today's movement for gay rights, I do not mean to equate the two. Nor is today's movement the same as the civil rights movement of the 1960s in which many of us participated as representatives of our Church. That we did so with the Church's blessing is itself an obvious difference. More obvious and profound are the differences between the experiences of lesbian and gay Americans who live or have lived in fear of disclosure and black Americans who must live daily and openly in the legacy left by slavery. At the same time, there is a similarity in the calls to counter acts of hate and discrimination experienced by members of both communities. We hear that call equally in the brutal deaths of both James Byrd Jr., a black man beaten and dragged along a gravel road in Jasper, Texas, and Matthew Shepard, a gay man beaten and lashed to a fence outside of Laramie, Wyoming. But we can also hear the call to resistance in those official pronouncements of the Church which are demeaning and hurtful to a class of people and inflict psychological harm.

We need to continue our participation in the ongoing civil rights movement of African Americans and we need to acknowledge the movement for human rights for gay, lesbian,

bisexual, and transgendered persons. The movement for gay
rights is for all concerned people. Those opposed prefer to see it
not as a movement but as an "agenda" of a group of sinners
seeking special privilege. Those of us who do see it as a human
rights movement in our society are painfully aware that the
institutional church has not only failed to support its gay and
lesbian members in their societal struggle, but in word and deed
has been among their most hurtful adversaries.

2) Those who are most hurt by the Judicial Council ruling
are lesbian and gay United Methodists, baptized and received
into church membership, and now denied the next traditional
form of sacramental blessing.

The overriding witness of homosexual persons is that their
sexual orientation is not a matter of choice. They can choose,
however, to faithfully and responsibly join in a holy covenant
with another person whom they love. If they are United
Methodists and they seek the Church's blessing and support in
their commitment to love, cherish, and uphold one another, they
have been turned away by official church action. By denying the
possibility of a committed relationship between two people of
the same gender who truly love each other, the Church actually
encourages a stereotype of gay promiscuity. The Church also
displays once again, as it has so often in its history, its fear and
ignorance of human sexuality.

The Church, of course, gives mixed messages to members of
the gay community. In Madison, Wisconsin, there are several
churches of different denominations who have publicly declared
themselves open and welcoming to lesbians and gays, including
one reconciling congregation of The United Methodist Church.
Since 1996 these churches have at various times been picketed
on Sunday mornings by members of a group calling themselves
"Wisconsin Christians United." They appear with placards
damning gays and lesbians to hell, distribute inflammatory
leaflets to those coming to worship, and videotape their car
license plates. This group has also placed its message of hate on
large billboards at several points in the city. (These have been
removed after a large public outcry.)

The coalition of welcoming churches invited the Reverend

Mel White to Madison for a public lecture. He is on the national staff of the Fellowship of Metropolitan Community Churches, but formerly was a speechwriter for Jerry Falwell and Pat Robertson. At a breakfast meeting with clergy he challenged them to draft a statement which would be a clear word of affirmation to the lesbian and gay community. The result was "A Madison Affirmation on Homosexuality and the Christian Faith." I was part of a representative drafting committee, and the statement was signed by over sixty clergy from ten denominations. The "Madison Affirmation" later ran as a paid advertisement with additional signatures, setting off a war of words in the Madison newspapers.

Wisconsin Christians United responded by distributing leaflets in the home neighborhoods of clergy who signed the Affirmation. For instance under a headline, "A Wolf on the Loose in Madison???", the flyer distributed in my neighborhood specifically named me a false prophet who comes as a wolf in sheep's clothing, citing Matthew 7:15 and six more supporting Bible verses. To the delight of us clergy-signers, the flyer also printed the full text of the Madison Affirmation, giving it wider circulation and garnering phone calls of support from our Jewish, Christian, and secular neighbors.

The Madison Affirmation is intentionally a statement of Christian clergy who think it important to speak clearly and pointedly over against the anti-gay assertions of a group whose name presumptively suggests it speaks for all Christians. The statement also was a means of countering the wishy-washy ambiguities of our respective denominations. Here is how the Madison Affirmation began:

> Jesus Christ calls us to love God and neighbor as ourselves. As Christian clergy we embrace gay and lesbian persons as our neighbors. From our reading of scripture and from our pastoral experiences, we believe there is sufficient evidence to conclude that homosexuality is neither sickness nor sin. For too long, homosexual persons have been condemned and mistreated by the followers of Jesus Christ. Sadly, the Bible has been misused in support of this condemnation. This abuse of scripture must end. Heterosexual and homosexual persons are children of God, created in God's image. We invite Christians to prayerfully re-

examine scripture and their consciences for any vestiges of hatred or prejudice against their homosexual brothers and sisters.
[The full text of the Madison Affirmation appears in Appendix D.]

It goes on to include an acknowledgment of the church's sin and arrogance and words of gratitude to gay and lesbian Christians who have remained in the church.

The Madison Affirmation speaks that word of truth and grace which the gay and lesbian community needs to hear from the church. I would encourage clergy in other communities to act similarly. Clear and forthright words can be a form of resistance over against the doublespeak of most denominations on this issue. Needless to say, in working on the Madison Affirmation I was embarrassed by the stance of my own denomination, as were others of theirs. I found, however, ecumenical support and gained an admiration for clergy of other denominations who seemed more free to think and act than most United Methodists.

3) The Judicial Council decision works to limit and undermine the ministry of pastors who extend the love of Christ, and develop trust and support within the gay community.

Developing and conducting services of holy union is both pastoral counseling and priestly celebration. Through these services the Church affirms individuals in their deepest concern for each other. These rituals become a means for a community to express its joy in God's love, which conquers the fears they know all too well.

Such services allow the families of gays and lesbians to experience the Church's affirmation of their sons, daughters, and siblings. Many parents find it hard to share their gay and lesbian children's lives with others, not knowing the response they will receive. I found that when I specifically included concern for homosexual persons in prayers or sermons it was an invitation for family members to confide in me. Sometimes this led to families of gays and lesbians coming to know and support each other. Services of holy union can be open family celebrations, increasing acceptance and healing. In this way, too, these services are pastoral ministry.

In 1975–76 I was on a committee which developed a book to illustrate how ritual could be used in ministering to people in significant experiences in their lives. The book, *Ritual in a New Day*, was published by the General Board of Discipleship's Section on Worship. It was that part of the Alternate Rituals Project which addressed nonofficial rituals and was an invitation to explore the use of ritual as ministry to people in various transitions in their lives.

Ritual in a New Day came under fire because one of its chapters addressed the use of ritual with persons who were divorcing. The chapter carefully stated that it was not advocating divorce but acknowledging that divorced persons are a part of every one of our congregations. Is there a way that the Church can be openly helpful and healing, using ritual as a means for a couple and a congregation to move gracefully into a new relationship? There was, of course, newspaper coverage of the book which erroneously stated that The United Methodist Church now had a Rite of Divorce. There followed a response of shock and horror from some United Methodists who had read the newspaper but not the book. The Judicial Council was called upon to affirm, even as the book stated, that these were not official rites of the Church, which can only be adopted by General Conference.

The book did affirm, however, that ritual acts can be a form of ministry and a significantly helpful means of responding to important life situations. Pastors have not been limited to the performance of only the official rites of the Church and many have creatively and compassionately responded to the spiritual needs of their congregation through special acts of worship. Rituals of holy union are a form of ministry which the Church can and should extend to its lesbian and gay members who seek to make a life commitment to each other, undergirded by their faith in Jesus Christ and their desire for the Church's blessing.

The 1996 General Conference added this statement to the Social Principles: "Ceremonies that celebrate homosexual unions shall not be conducted by our ministers and shall not be conducted in our churches" (65C). Yet the Preface to the Social Principles defines its nature this way: "[The Social Principles] are intended to be instructive and persuasive in the best of the prophetic spirit. The Social Principles are a call to all members of The United Methodist Church to a prayerful, studied dialogue of faith and practice."

There is an obvious conflict in these two statements, creating a dilemma for pastors who differ with the ban on holy unions. Is the "shall not" language binding within Social Principles which are, by self-definition, advisory ("intended to be instructive")? The Judicial Council, sidestepping the nature of the Social Principles, ruled narrowly that pastors conducting "celebrations of homosexual union" (not defined) were subject to charges and trial. The Social Principles thereby moved from inviting healthy discourse and debate to promoting perpetual acts of divisive trial and recrimination, as seems now to be the case. Unfortunately, such partisan vindictiveness seems to be the current spirit of American politics and government. Instead of seeking to heal our country's cultural civil war, the 1996 General Conference only added fuel to the fires, with our church trials gaining national media coverage.

United Methodists learn how to live with their Social Principles, which are amended every four years. When we disagree with a statement we join in a continuing dialogue, allowing each other the right to differ. We recognized that bans on thought are contrary to human nature. However, this new Social Principle differs from others in that it places an enforceable ban on a particular action, indeed on an act of ministry. The General Conference action and the Judicial Council's decision combined to contravene in the pastoral ministry of conscientious and compassionate United Methodist pastors. On this ground alone they deserve to be resisted.

I value my ordination and my call to Christian ministry, which has included working with gay and lesbian couples as they plan services of holy union and lives of committed love. I shall continue to do so when I am asked. There are many United Methodist clergy who have indicated they are available to conduct these services, in spite of the Council's ruling. We retired clergy report our pastoral activity once a year. I, along with others, will be reporting the number of "marriages and holy unions" I have conducted, as one category. It's time for holy unions to be counted because they are significant events in lives that count to God, if not to the institutional church.

The United Methodist Church will change. It may become ever more rigid, doctrinaire, and inquisitorial. I hope not! Rather, I hope that United Methodist pastors will be free to openly minister to their lesbian and gay constituents in good conscience, unthreatened, and without recrimination. I pray that The United Methodist Church will cease hurting its gay and lesbian members, and indeed learn compassion from them. I look forward to that time when, in their struggle for human rights, lesbians and gays will find United Methodists to be "friendly to liberty."

Conclusion

Amy E. DeLong

Razing the Roof

As I was trying to bring clarity to my final thoughts, my mind kept wandering to the passage in Mark's Gospel about the man who couldn't walk who was carried by his friends to a house where Jesus was. The friends, unable to get through the crowd and bring the man to Jesus, got up on top of the house and removed the roof so that he could be lowered in from above. I think about this passage because this is the kind of bold action that needs to be taken on behalf of our gay and lesbian brothers and sisters. When there are too many people blocking the entrance of the church, the roof needs to be torn off, giving open access to all who have been paralyzed by the church's proscriptions.

As people of faith, we must hear the voice of God calling for a new way. I am reminded of Walter Brueggemann's words "We are God's people. We have eaten at God's table. We have heard God's word. We are identified as the odd ones of the world, called to be at odds with the world, ordained to call into question the world's way of doing business."[1]

Tex and I want to be very clear that our desire in bringing this book to the Church was not to add fuel to an already out-of-control fire or to drive the wedge dividing The United Methodist Church even deeper. Our desire was to give voice to

192

some of the many United Methodists who believe that our cat-
egorical exclusion of gays and lesbians from full participation in
the life of the Church needs to be changed. We believe we have
provided that voice. In this one volume we have brought together contributors from all walks of The United Methodist Church
who are in solidarity with gay and lesbian Christians and who
are working hard to bring about better days. Together we have
shown that homosexuality is not about an "issue." It is about
people, God's people, who are wounded in profound ways by
the Church's limitations and rejection. Those who are suffering
and battle-weary long to come home to that place where they
are seen as precious *because* of who they are and where they can
experience God's unconditional love. We hope this work helps
move our denomination in the direction to become that place.

Most important, we undertook this project because we love
The United Methodist Church—and we know it can be better
than it is. It can speak more prophetically; it can love more
inclusively; it can listen more compassionately; it can act more
justly. We know that it can. It is our prayer that it will.

As I have spent time during the past two years working on
this book, I have heard many of the arguments leveled against
us. But, I continued to find one refrain particularly stinging—
and that is that we (that is, all who are considered the loyal
opposition) have an "agenda."

I began to feel better about this accusation only after I realized that some people have gotten the word "agenda" confused
with the word "gospel." It is not an agenda when we try to be
in ministry to and with all of God's children, when we say our
love ought to be as inclusive as we claim God's love is, when we
try to make room for everyone at Christ's table. This is not an
agenda. It is the gospel.

Our actions are neither a personal whim nor designed to further some undisclosed intention. We do not want to conquer or
displace dedicated people. We want only to live out the gospel
message of radical compassion as faithfully as we can—and
sometimes that means we are called to disagree with Church
law.

Even in the midst of our frustration, brokenness, anguish,

and anger, our hope lies in the understanding that God yearns for the Church's wholeness and healing. We sense God's transfiguring Spirit at work in many ways. We want to be a part of that Divine movement, where God's vision of grace and justice is prevailing. There is hope, but there is also much work ahead of us. I had an Old Testament professor who once said, "If you read the scriptures and feel comfortable, you have misunderstood them." Tex and I feel the same about this book. We want you to know there is hope, and yet be shaken and disquieted by all that needs to be done. We pray for courage and peace to all who are working creatively to help God's "kin-dom" be realized among us.

Note

1. *The Other Side* 35, no. 3 (May/June 1999): 8.

Appendix A

Frequently Cited Paragraphs from
The Book of Discipline of
The United Methodist Church

¶65C - *Marriage*

We affirm the sanctity of the marriage covenant that is expressed in love, mutual support, personal commitment, and shared fidelity between a man and a woman. We believe that God's blessing rests upon such marriage, whether or not there are children of the union. We reject social norms that assume different standards for women than for men in marriage. Ceremonies that celebrate homosexual unions shall not be conducted by our ministers and shall not be conducted in our churches.

¶65G - *Human Sexuality*

We recognize that sexuality is God's good gift to all persons. We believe persons may be fully human only when that gift is acknowledged and affirmed by themselves, the church, and society. We call all persons to the disciplined, responsible fulfillment of themselves, others, and society in the stewardship of this gift. We also recognize our limited understanding of this complex gift and encourage the medical, theological, and social science disciplines to combine in a determined effort to understand human sexuality more completely. We call the Church to take the leadership role in bringing together these disciplines to address this most complex issue. Further, within the context of our understanding of this gift of God, we recognize that God challenges us to find responsible, committed, and loving forms of expression.

Although all persons are sexual beings whether or not they are married, sexual relations are only clearly affirmed in the marriage bond. Sex may become expoitative within as well as outside marriage. We reject all sexual expressions that damage or destroy the humanity God has given us as birthright, and we affirm only that sexual expression which enhances that same humanity. We believe that sexual relations where one or both partners are exploitative, abusive, or promiscuous are beyond the parameters of acceptable Christian behavior and are ultimately destructive to individuals, families, and the social order.

We deplore all forms of commercialization and exploitation of sex, with their consequent cheapening and degradation of human personality. We call for strict enforcement of laws prohibiting the sexual exploitation or use of children by adults. We call for the establishment of adequate protective services, guidance, and counseling opportunities for children thus abused. We insist that all persons, regardless of age, gender, marital status, or sexual orientation, are entitled to have their human and civil rights ensured.

We recognize the continuing need for full, positive, and factual sex education opportunities for children, youth, and adults. The Church offers a unique opportunity to give quality guidance and education in this area.

Homosexual persons no less than heterosexual persons are individuals of sacred worth. All persons need the ministry and guidance of the church in their struggles for human fulfillment, as well as the spiritual and emotional care of a fellowship that enables reconciling relationships with God, with others, and with self. Although we do not condone the practice of homosexuality and consider this practice incompatible with Christian teaching, we affirm that God's grace is available to all. We commit ourselves to be in ministry for and with all persons.

¶66H - *Equal Rights Regardless of Sexual Orientation*

Certain basic human rights and civil liberties are due all persons. We are committed to supporting those rights and liberties for homosexual persons. We see a clear issue of simple justice in protecting their rightful claims where they have shared material resources, pensions, guardian relationships, mutual powers of attorney, and other such lawful claims typically attendant to contractual relationships that involve shared contributions, responsibilities, and liabilities, and equal protection before the law. Moreover, we support efforts to stop violence and other forms of coercion against gays and lesbians. We also commit ourselves to social witness against coercion and marginalization of former homosexuals.

¶304.3 - *Ordination*

While persons set apart by the Church for ordained ministry are subject to all the frailties of the human condition and the pressures of society, they are required to maintain the highest standards of holy living in the world. Since the practice of homosexuality is incompatible with Christian teaching, self-avowed practicing homosexuals are not to be accepted as candidates, ordained as ministers, or appointed to serve The United Methodist Church.

¶806.12 - *General Council on Finance and Administration—Fiscal Responsibility*

The council shall be responsible for ensuring that no board, agency, committee, commission, or council shall give United Methodist funds to any gay caucus or group, or otherwise use such funds to promote the acceptance of homosexuality. The council shall have the right to stop such expenditures. This restriction shall not limit the Church's ministry in response to the HIV epidemic.

Appendix B

1998 Judicial Council Ruling

The following is the August 1998 Judicial Council ruling regarding the conducting of same-gender covenanting ceremonies:

The prohibitive statement in Par. 65C of the *1996 Discipline:* "Ceremonies that celebrate homosexual unions shall not be conducted by our ministers and shall not be conducted in our churches," has the effect of church law, notwithstanding its placement in Par. 65C and, therefore, governs the conduct of the ministerial office. Conduct in violation of this prohibition renders clergy liable to a charge of disobedience to the Order and Discipline of The United Methodist Church under Par. 2624 of the *Discipline.*

Appendix C

Bishop Tuell's Response to the Greg Dell Case

Prior to General Conference 2000, Bishop Tuell, who presided over Greg Dell's trial, sent a letter to General Conference delegates urging them to repeal the prohibitions in *The Book of Discipline* against United Methodist clergy conducting same-gender union services.

In his letter to delegates, Bishop Tuell said, "After two long days of presiding over Rev. Dell's trial last March, I was totally convinced that the legislation of 1996 was not good legislation and should be changed by the 2000 General Conference."

He went on to say:

[T]he 1996 legislation violates the precious freedom which we have always believed our clergy to possess as 'men and women of God,' and subjects them to being 'defrocked' for their conscientious adherence to their high calling. This is wrong, and should be corrected. . . . The provisions of Par. 65C are likely to hit some of our most able, conscientious clergy the hardest. The 13 elders on the Trial Court in the Gregory Dell case, even though they quite appropriately found him guilty, made a separate statement affirming his outstanding ministry of 30 years. We cannot afford to lose men and women of this caliber. . . . I truly believe that the continuance of the 1996 legislation can have nothing but destructive and divisive effect across the connection, as well-publicized trials are held with varying and illogical results. United Methodism does not need this.

Appendix D

A Madison Affirmation
On Homosexuality and Christian Faith

Jesus Christ calls us to love God and our neighbor as ourselves. As Christian clergy we embrace gay and lesbian persons as our neighbors. From our reading of scripture and from our pastoral experiences, we believe there is sufficient evidence to conclude that homosexuality is neither sickness nor sin. For too long, homosexual persons have been condemned and mistreated by the followers of Jesus Christ. Sadly, the Bible has been misused in support of this condemnation. This abuse of scripture must end. Heterosexual and homosexual persons are children of God, created in God's image. We invite Christians to prayerfully reexamine scripture and their consciences for any vestiges of hatred or prejudice against their homosexual brothers and sisters.

We strongly uphold the family as the basic social unit in which we are called to live together and to give and receive nurture and support. We often find the term "family values" applied to only some Christian families. Gay and lesbian persons live among us as our brothers and sisters, fathers and mothers, sons and daughters, uncles and aunts, nephews and nieces. We believe in the value of loving, committed families for all God's children. We support families who provide love and affirmation for each of their members. We are saddened and concerned by the breakdown of the family that stems from various forms of infidelity, violence, and failure to maintain long-term loving commitments among both heterosexual and homosexual communities. We commit ourselves to the encouragement and blessing of relationships that meet the test of fidelity and loving nurture.

We believe it is time to eliminate all policies and practices which create barriers and restrictions to the full participation of gay and lesbian Christians in all of the privileges and responsibilities of church membership. Recognizing that our churches still speak and act out of our long-standing prejudices:

- ❑ we hope and pray that we will acknowledge our sin and be forgiven for our ignorance, fear, arrogance and self-righteousness;
- ❑ we commit ourselves and encourage others to engage in the study of scripture and open dialogue with other disciplines to allow the Holy Spirit to teach new understanding;
- ❑ we rejoice in the refusal of many gay and lesbian Christians to abandon or be forced out of their church homes;
- ❑ we are moved by their gracious response to years of intolerance and inspired by their creative and courageous service to the gospel of Jesus Christ;
- ❑ we consider these sisters and brothers to be a unique, holy, and precious gift to all of us who struggle to become the family of God.

We hope and pray that those who have left our churches will in God's time return to full and unqualified membership in the Christian community and by their presence help us to be renewed as the church of Jesus Christ.

Contributors

Gilbert Haven Caldwell is currently the minister of Church and Community at Park Hill United Methodist Church in Denver, Colorado. He has served as a pastor in Massachusetts, Connecticut, New York (Brooklyn and Harlem), and Pennsylvania; as a campus minister; as a district superintendent; and as a staff member of the United Methodist Commission on Religion and Race.

Ignacio Castuera is pastor at the North Glendale United Methodist Church, Glendale, California. He has served churches in Hawaii, Los Angeles, and Hollywood. While serving churches in Los Angeles he was executive director of All Nations Foundation. He also worked at UCLA as a counseling psychologist. In 1980 he became the first Latino district superintendent of the Los Angeles District. Dr. Castuera has taught and lectured in many settings and has written many articles in professional journals.

Amy E. DeLong is an ordained United Methodist clergywoman currently serving churches in the Wisconsin Annual Conference. She earned a Master of Divinity from Garrett-Evangelical Theological Seminary and a Master of Arts in Theology from United Theological Seminary of the Twin Cities.

E. Dale Dunlap is Academic Dean and Professor of Theology Emeritus of Saint Paul School of Theology in Kansas City, Missouri, where he taught United Methodist history, doctrine, and polity. He is a retired member of Kansas West Annual Conference, which he represented in three general conferences and six jurisdictional conferences. He chaired the 1980–1984 Ministry Study Committee and was a member and editorial writer for the 1988–1996 Committee to Study Baptism.

Victor Paul Furnish is University Distinguished Professor of New

Testament in Southern Methodist University's Perkins School of Theology. He is a clergy member of the Northern Illinois Conference and a former president of the Society of Biblical Literature. Dr. Furnish is the author of many biblical commentaries, books, articles, and reviews. In addition to his own publications he is General Editor and Chair of the Editorial Board of the twenty-volume Abingdon New Testament Commentaries series.

Leontine T. C. Kelly served as Resident Bishop San Francisco Area and the president of Western Jurisdiction College of Bishops. In 1984, she was the second female and first African American woman to be elected bishop of any major denomination. Prior to the episcopacy she served local churches in Virginia, was Associate Program Council Director of the Virginia Annual Conference, and became Assistant General Secretary in the area of evangelism for the United Methodist General Board of Discipleship.

John Kruse is a retired United Methodist clergymember of the Wisconsin Annual Conference, where he has served since 1956. He resides in Madison where his wife has been on the academic staff of the University of Wisconsin since 1976. They have three daughters and two grandchildren whom they love and respect.

Susan Laurie lives with her partner Julie and is very thankful for this relationship. Responding to God's call to ministry, Susan left teaching and earned a Master of Divinity degree from Garrett-Evangelical Theological Seminary. She seeks ordination in the Western Pennsylvania Annual Conference.

Joretta L. Marshall is Associate Professor in Pastoral Care and Counseling and is Associate Dean at Iliff School of Theology in Denver, Colorado. She is an Ordained Elder in the Rocky Mountain Annual Conference.

Terry L. Norman is an ordained United Methodist clergyperson who took early retirement from the church in 1990 after voluntarily disclosing his gay orientation. He is the cofounder of the Norman Institute, a nonprofit, educational corporation focusing on issues related to gender orientation, located in Kansas City, Missouri.

L. Edward Phillips is Associate Professor of Historical Theology and Dean of the Chapel at Garrett-Evangelical Theological Seminary in Evanston, Illinois. He is an Ordained Elder in the Memphis Annual Conference and has served churches in Georgia, Tennessee, and Indiana. His professional interests include the history of theology and worship and the intersection between liturgy and ethics.

Jeanne Audrey Powers is a prominent ecumenist and advocate of women's rights. She served for many years as the Associate General Commission on Christian Unity and Interreligious Concerns. She is a member of the Minnesota Annual Conference and was elected to one General Conference and four Jurisdictional Conferences. She was the first woman in the Church to receive votes for bishop. She retired in 1996, after 38 years in the ordained ministry.

Tex Sample is a freelance lecturer, consultant, and author. He is the Robert B. and Kathleen Rogers Professor of Church and Society Emeritus at Saint Paul School of Theology in Kansas City, Missouri. He resides with his spouse Peggy in Phoenix, Arizona.

Roy I. Sano is currently bishop of the Los Angeles Area, California-Pacific Conference. Bishop Sano has also served the Denver area, including the Rocky Mountain and Yellowstone Conferences. Prior to the episcopacy, he served in various pastoral roles and academic settings. He was Professor of Theology and Pacific and Asian American Ministries at Pacific School of Religion, Berkeley, California, when he was elected to the episcopacy in 1984.

Barbara B. Troxell is Associate Professor of Practical Theology and Director of Field Education and Spiritual Formation at Garrett-Evangelical Theological Seminary in Evanston, Illinois. She is a United Methodist clergywoman who has served in parish, campus, administrative, and seminary forms of ministry for forty years.

Dwight W. Vogel is Professor of Theology and Ministry and Director of the Nellie B. Ebersole Program in Sacred Music at Garrett-Evangelical Theological Seminary in Evanston, Illinois, where he coordinates the M.A. in music ministry and Ph.D. in liturgical studies degree programs. He is a member of the Order of Saint Luke, which he serves as Abbot. Dr. Vogel is an ordained elder of The United Methodist Church.

J. Philip Wogaman is senior minister at the historic Foundry United Methodist Church and longtime professor of Christian Ethics at Wesley Theological Seminary, Washington, D.C. Author of many books relating Christian faith to ethics, he has also been a leader in The United Methodist Church. In 2000 he will serve for the fourth time as delegate to the General Conference. He is a member of the Baltimore-Washington Annual Conference.